THE COMING OF CHRIST

THE COMING

Produced by LOOK *Magazine Book Division/Based on the NBC Project 20 television production*

The inspiring story of the prophecy, birth and message of Jesus Christ as seen through the eyes of the great masters and told in the words of the Old and New Testaments

OF CHRIST

Richard Hanser and Donald B. Hyatt, with Foreword by Dr. Ralph W. Sockman

Published by Cowles Magazines and Broadcasting, Inc., New York, N.Y./Book trade distribution by Doubleday and Company, Inc., Garden City, New York

LOOK Magazine Book Division / Cowles Magazines and Broadcasting, Inc.

Gardner Cowles, *Editor & President*   Marvin C. Whatmore, *General Manager*

Gilbert C. Maurer, *Manager Book Division*

THE COMING OF CHRIST

Designer: Leonard Jossel • *Research Associates:* Helen Buttfield, Daniel Selznick

CONTENTS

FOREWORD

Religious faith should not outrage reason, but it does outrun reason. The more we know, the more we realize the range of life beyond our knowledge. Our science is but an island of charted facts in the ocean of the unknown. The larger the island grows, the longer the shoreline of mystery. Albert Einstein said that the most beautiful thing we can experience is the mysterious. It is the source of all true art and science. And he added that the person to whom this emotion is a stranger, who can no longer pause to wonder and stand rapt in awe, is as good as dead; his eyes are closed.

Religious faith stirs feelings too deep for words, feelings that break through language and escape. We cannot confine the infinite God in creeds, nor explain the sublimity of Christ in definitions. But the painter's brush captures that which eludes the writer's pen. It seeks to present the ideal world beyond the reach of the photographer's lens. The true artist experiences the answer to Saint Paul's prayer: May God grant you the spirit of wisdom and revelation for the knowledge of Himself, illuminating the eyes of your heart. (Ephesians 1:17-18).

It is not strange that many of the great artists have so largely found their inspiration and their themes in the Bible. The Judaeo-Christian Scriptures opened the deepest springs of feeling and the highest sources of hope. Greek art portrayed the forms and figures of this world with a grace never yet surpassed, but Christian art reached for the infinite and the eternal. It conceived man as an immortal soul and essayed to portray life that is too great for the grave, love that is too strong for death.

From the fourteenth to the end of the seventeenth century, Europe's artists gave themselves to portraying the origins and promises of their religious faith which run beyond this earthly realm. It was this period which produced the majority of the masterpieces of painting presented in this book as a narrative of the Christian story.

The nineteenth century with its emphasis on the scientific spirit determined to show its sincerity by stripping art of its imaginative element and limiting it more to the factual. But truth is more than mere facts, as spiritual insight recognizes. And the representational art of the nineteenth century failed to match the religious portrayals of its predecessors.

Twentieth century painting has unleashed the imagination but it has largely lost the deep feeling for God essential to great religious art.

The early Christian artists opened the Holy Scriptures to the illiterate. Their paintings were the Bible for the people who could not read. Now the widespread presentation of great religious art bids fair to reopen the Bible to our age of more universal intellectual achievement. An increasing number of persons feel themselves educated beyond the range of conventional contemporary preaching. But when they ponder a religious masterpiece, their minds are started on trails of thought limited only by their own intelligence and imagination. They become explorers of the spirit. And if they look intently enough, they begin to feel intensely.

The most heart-warming, soul-stirring, life-changing personality in history is Jesus of Nazareth. In unparalleled fashion, His life has inspired artists to greatness in their efforts to portray Him. In the pages which follow are the works of forty-three painters selected with masterly discrimination. Through these windows of wonder the eye follows "the old, old story." We glimpse the law and the prophets that preceded the coming of Christ's love, the wondering look of Mary as she receives the divine annunciation, the haunting beauty of the Bethlehem scenes, the call and baptism of the Carpenter, the healing power of the Great Physician, the disciples listening to the matchless Teacher.

As we look at the Christ, we feel ourselves being looked at. We cease judging the painter's art, and find ourselves being judged by the artist's subject.

RALPH W. SOCKMAN

Pastor Emeritus,
Christ Church, Methodist, New York

THE LAND OF ISRAEL:
A timeless land,
where, *"a thousand years*
are but as yesterday
when it is past, and as a
watch in the night."
This is Holy Land, where
the word of God
was made manifest.

This is the land that received
the Law, written on tables of stone
by the finger of God and handed
down to Moses on Mt. Sinai.

Here it was written: "*Your old men
shall dream dreams, your young
men shall see visions.*" And here the
prophets of ancient Israel first
saw the vision of a coming Messiah who
one day would redeem the world.

"Behold!" said Isaiah, "a virgin shall conceive, and bear a son... And His name shall be called Wonderful, Counsellor, the Mighty God, the Everlasting Father, the Prince of Peace."

12

And in the fullness of time, this Land of Promise saw the marvel of His coming.

And the angel Gabriel
was sent from God unto a city
of Galilee, named Nazareth,
to a virgin espoused to a man
whose name was Joseph,
of the house of David; and
the virgin's name was Mary.

And the angel came in unto her, and said: *"Hail,*
thou that art highly favoured, the Lord
is with thee. Blessed art thou among women."

And when she saw him, she was troubled
at his saying, and cast in her mind what manner
of salutation this should be.

And the angel said unto her:
*"Fear not, Mary; for thou hast
found favour with God.*

*"And behold, thou shalt
bring forth a son, and shalt
call His name Jesus.*

*"He shall be called Great, and
shall be called the Son of
the Highest. And of His Kingdom
there shall be no end."*

Then said Mary unto the angel:
*"How shall this be,
seeing I know not a man?"*

And the angel answered, and said unto her: *"The Holy Ghost shall come upon thee, and the power of the Highest shall overshadow thee: therefore also that Holy Thing which shall be born of thee shall be called the Son of God."*

20

And Mary said : "*My soul doth magnify the Lord, and my spirit hath rejoiced in God my Saviour. For He hath regarded the low estate of His handmaiden ; for, behold, from henceforth all generations shall call me blessed.*"

21

All this happened in an obscure
district of a small out-of-the-way province
under the rulership of Imperial Rome.
And it came to pass in those days
that there went out a decree from
Caesar Augustus, that all the world should
be taxed, every one into his own city.

And Joseph also went up from Galilee,
out of the city of Nazareth, into Judaea,
unto the city of David, which is called
Bethlehem (because he was of the house and
lineage of David) to be taxed with Mary,
his espoused wife, being great with child.

Βut in Bethlehem, there was
no room for them at the inn.

23

And so it was, that, while they were there, the days were accomplished that Mary should be delivered.

And she brought forth her first-born son, and wrapped
Him in swaddling clothes, and laid Him in a manger.

As the angel
had commanded,
they called His name
Jesus: for He
would save His people
from their sins.

And there were in the same country
shepherds, abiding in the field, keeping
watch over their flock by night.

And, lo, the angel of the Lord came upon
them, and the glory of the Lord shone
round about them, and they were sore afraid.

And the angel said unto them:
*"Fear not, for, behold, I bring you good tidings
of great joy, which shall be to all people.*

*"For unto you is born this day, in the city
of David, a Saviour, which is Christ the Lord.*

*"And this shall be a sign unto you:
Ye shall find the Babe wrapped in swaddling
clothes, lying in a manger."*

And suddenly there was with the angel a multitude of the heavenly host, praising God and saying: *"Glory to God in the highest, and on earth peace, good will toward men."*

And the shepherds came with haste,
and found Mary and Joseph,
and the Babe lying in the manger.
And they worshipped Him,

glorifying and praising God
for all the things that they had
heard and seen, which the
Lord had made known unto them.

But Mary kept all these things, and pondered them in her heart.

N ow when Jesus was born in Bethlehem, there came Wise Men from the East seeking Him. For they had seen a strange, new star in the heavens, and they followed it.

And the Wise Men came
to Jerusalem to the court of
Herod the Great to inquire
*"Where is He that is born
King of the Jews? For we have
seen His star in the East
and are come to worship Him."*

But Herod was much troubled
to hear of a new King who
might displace him. *"When you
find him,"* he said, *"return
and tell me of it that I may
worship Him also."* But
Herod meant to destroy Him.

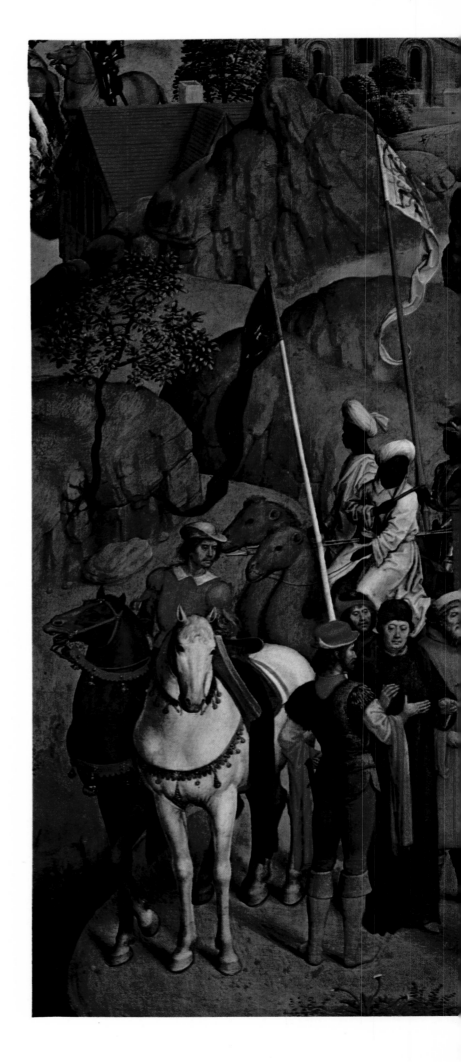

And so, the Wise Men continued their search. And lo, the star, which they saw in the East, went before them, till it came and stood over where the young Child was. And when they saw the young Child with Mary, His mother, they fell down, and worshipped Him.

And they opened their treasures and presented
unto Him gifts: gold, and frankincense, and myrrh.

Aund being warned of God not to return to Herod, they departed into their own country another way.

And the angel of the Lord appeared to Joseph in a dream, saying: *"Arise, and take the young Child and flee into Egypt, and be thou there until I bring thee word: For Herod will seek the young Child to destroy Him."*

So Joseph took the Child and His mother by night, and departed into Egy

. And Herod knew it not.

And Herod, in his
rage at being deceived by the
Wise Men, ordered his
soldiers to slay all children
in Bethlehem two years
old and under, thinking to
destroy Jesus among them.

48

Then was fulfilled
that which was spoken by
Jeremiah the prophet.

There was lamentation
and weeping, and great
mourning: Rachel weeping
for her children, and
would not be comforted,
because they were no more.

But far away, with His mother in the land of Egypt, the Child Jesus was safe from harm.

After a time, an angel of the Lord appeared in a dream to Joseph in Egypt, saying: *"Take the young Child and His mother, and go into the land of Israel. For they are dead which sought the young Child's life."* So Joseph, with Mary and the Child, returned to the land of Israel, into Galilee, to dwell in the city of Nazareth.

There, the childhood years of Jesus were passed in the home of His good father, Joseph, who was a carpenter.

And the Child grew, and waxed strong in spirit :

nd the grace of God was upon Him.

The years
passed, and the
boy Jesus
began to learn
the craft
of the carpenter
from His
father Joseph.

Now He was twelve years of age, and
the time had come for Him to make a memorable
journey. His parents, being devout Jews,
took Him to Jerusalem, ninety miles away, to
observe the Feast of the Passover.

And in the great city, He became separated from them. And they sought Him everywhere.

And it came to pass, that after three days, they found Him in the temple, sitting in the midst of the doctors, both hearing them and asking them questions.

And all that heard
Him were astonished
at His understanding
and His answers.

67

When his parents saw Him, they were amazed: and His mother said unto Him: *"Son, Thy father and I have sought Thee sorrowing."*

And He said unto them: *"Knew ye not that I must be about My Father's business*

And they understood not the saying which He spake unto them.

And from that time,
Jesus increased
in wisdom and stature,
and in favour
with God and man.

70

But of the next eighteen years of His life on earth, nothing was recorded.

Now among the people of the Land of Israel, after a silence of more than four hundred years, a new prophet arose who spake as Isaiah and Jeremiah had spoken before him.

It was the voice of one crying in the wilderness, and saying: *"Prepare ye the way of the Lord; make His paths straight."*

His name was John the Baptist.

And there went out unto him all the land of Judaea, and they of Jerusalen

nd were all baptized of him in the river of Jordan, confessing their sins.

And as the people were in expectation, all men mused in their hearts whether or not John were the Christ, the Messiah.

But John answered, saying unto them all: "*I indeed baptize you with water; but One mightier than I cometh, the latchet of whose shoes I am not worthy to unloose. He shall baptize you with the Holy Ghost and with fire.*"

Then Jesus Himself, though
sinless, came to the Jordan
to be baptized in dedication
for His coming ministry.

And Jesus, when He was
baptized, went up straightway
out of the water; and
lo, the heavens were opened
unto Him, and He saw
the Spirit of God descending
like a dove, and lighting
upon Him. And lo, a voice
came from heaven, saying:
*"This is my beloved Son, in
whom I am well pleased."*

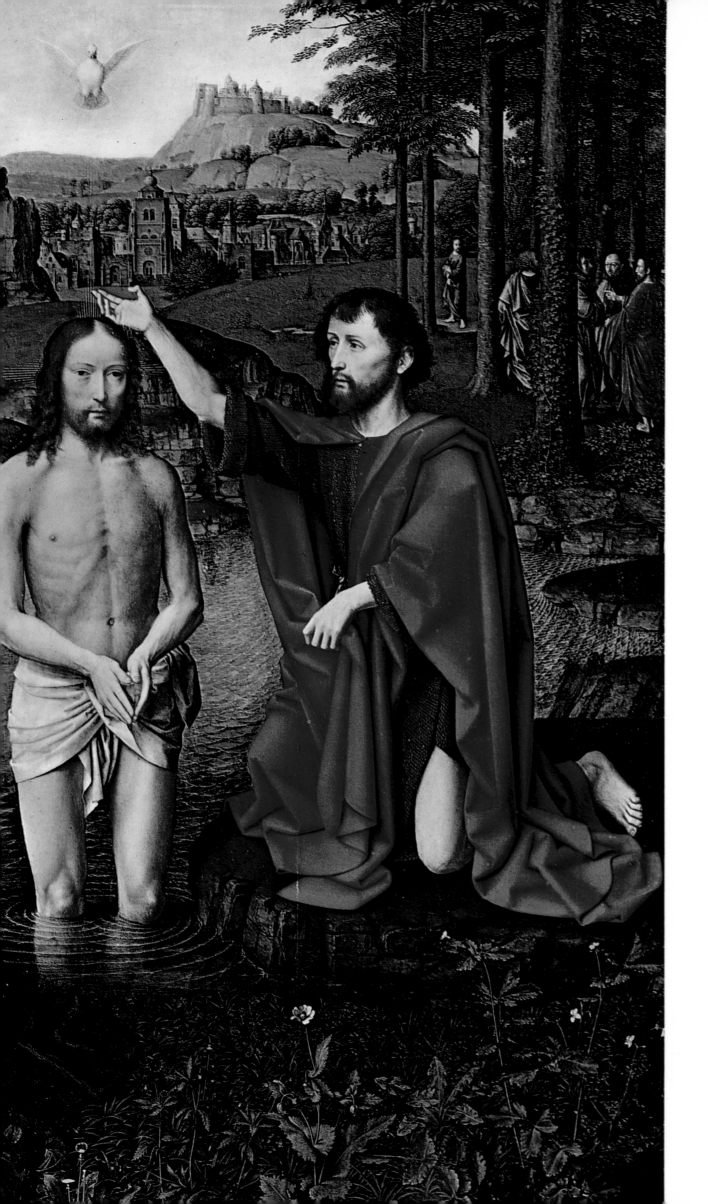

And Jesus was
about thirty years
of age as His
ministry began.

And it came to pass afterward, that He went throughout every city and village, preaching the glad tidings of the Kingdom of God. And the common people heard Him gladly.

He said: "*I am the light of the world: He that followeth Me shall not walk in darkness, but shall have the light of life.*"

And He said: "*Thou shalt love the Lord thy God with all thy heart, and with all thy soul, and with all thy mind. This is the first and great commandment.*

"And the second is like unto it: Thou shalt love thy neighbour as thyself. On these two commandments hang all the Law and the prophets."

And when they questioned Him, asking when the Kingdom
of God should come, He answered them, saying:
"The Kingdom of God cometh not with observation.
Neither shall they say, Lo here! or Lo there!
For Behold, the Kingdom of God is within you."

He asked them: *"What shall it profit a man if he shall*
gain the whole world, and lose his own soul?"

They called Him 'rabbi' (which is to say 'teacher')
and it was said of Him: "*Of a truth, this is the Prophet.*"
And there went out a fame of Him through all the region.

When the sabbath day was come,
He began to teach in the synagogue:
and many hearing Him were astonished,
saying, *"From whence hath this man
these things?"* And: *"What wisdom is this
which is given unto him? Is not
this the carpenter, the son of Mary?"*
And they were offended at Him.

Still others mocked,
saying: *"Out of Galilee
ariseth no prophet."*

Now Jesus, walking by the
Sea of Galilee, saw two brethren,
Simon called Peter, and Andrew
his brother, casting a net into
the sea, for they were fishers.

And He said unto them: *"Follow Me,
and I will make you fishers of men."*

And they straightway left their
nets, and followed Him.

95

He ordained twelve to be with Him. And He gave them power and authorit

er all devils, and to cure diseases. And He sent them to preach the Kingdom of God.

And they departed, and went through
the towns, preaching the gospel
and healing everywhere: James the son
of Zebedee; Philip and Bartholomew;
Thomas, and Matthew the publican; James
the son of Alphaeus, and Lebbaeus
whose surname was Thaddeus; Simon
the Canaanite, and Judas Iscariot;
who would also betray Him...

Andrew, who said: *"We have
found the Messias, which is being
interpreted, the Christ..."*

…John, 'the disciple whom Jesus loved;'

And Simon, who is called Peter, the brother of Andrew.

102

From the beginning, they were 'eyewitnesses and ministers of His word.' And they were astonished at His doctrine, for He taught them as One having authority, and not as the scribes.

"The works that I do," He said, "bear witness of Me, that the Father hath sent Me." And the whole multitude sought to touch Him: for there went virtue out of Him, healing them all.

MANY believed in His name when they saw the miracles which He did. And they said, *"Of a truth*

hou art the Son of God." All men did marvel at His deeds, and were astonished with a great astonishment.

His words fell like balm on the afflicted. He would say: *"Be of good comfort. Thy faith hath made thee whole. Go in peace."* Or: *"Rise, take up thy bed and walk."*

Since the world began,
it was not heard that
any man opened the eyes
of one that was born blind.

"No man," they said, "can do these miracles
that Thou doest, except God be with Him." And they
brought unto Him all sick people that were
taken with divers diseases and torments, and those
which were possessed with devils, and those
which were lunatick, and those that had the palsy.

And He healed them.

112

His disciples rebuked those that brought
them. But when Jesus saw it, He was
much displeased, and said unto them: *"Suffer the
little children to come unto Me, and forbid
them not. For of such is the Kingdom of God . . .*

"Verily I say unto you,
except ye be converted and
become as little children,
ye shall not enter into
the Kingdom of Heaven."

And He put His hands upon
them, and blessed them.

And He said: "Whoso shall receive one such little child in My name receiveth Me."

"I speak not of Myself, but the Father that dwelleth in Me: He doeth the good works."

1 from beyond Jordan, there followed great multitudes of people to hear Him speak.

And seeing the multitudes, He went up into a mountai

And when He was set, His disciples came unto Him.

And He opened His mouth, and taught them, saying...

126

"Blessed are the poor in spirit:
for theirs is the Kingdom of Heaven...

"Blessed are they that mourn:
for they shall be comforted …

"Blessed are the meek: for they shall inherit the earth...

"Blessed are the merciful: for they shall obtain mercy...

133

"Blessed are the pure in heart: for they shall see God.

"Blessed are the peacemakers: for they shall be called the children of God."

And on the Mount,
He pronounced the rule
of life which coming
generations would call 'golden.'

He said: *"Therefore all things whatsoever ye would that men should do to you, do ye even so to them."*

Thus He spoke and thus He taught in the little land of Israel two thousand years ago, and His words changed the hearts of men around the world.

Of Him it was written : *"For the Law was given by Moses, but grace and truth came by Jesus Christ."*

His law was love. To His disciples,
for all mankind, He said: *"A new
commandment I give unto you, that ye
love one another: As I have loved
you, that ye also love one another."*

142

THE COMING OF CHRIST

The Scriptures according to the King James Version of the Holy Bible

ISAIAH 53

LUKE 1 and 2

MATTHEW 1 through 7

WHO hath believed our report? and to whom is the arm of the Lord revealed?

2 For he shall grow up before him as a tender plant, and as a root out of a dry ground: he hath no form nor comeliness; and when we shall see him, there is no beauty that we should desire him.

3 He is despised and rejected of men; a man of sorrows, and acquainted with grief: and we hid as it were our faces from him; he was despised, and we esteemed him not.

4 Surely he hath borne our griefs, and carried our sorrows: yet we did esteem him stricken, smitten of God, and afflicted.

5 But he was wounded for our transgressions, he was bruised for our iniquities: the chastisement of our peace was upon him; and with his stripes we are healed.

6 All we like sheep have gone astray; we have turned every one to his own way; and the Lord hath laid on him the iniquity of us all.

7 He was oppressed, and he was afflicted, yet he opened not his mouth: he is brought as a lamb to the slaughter, and as a sheep before her shearers is dumb, so he openeth not his mouth.

8 He was taken from prison and from judgment: and who shall declare his generation? for he was cut off out of the land of the living: for the transgression of my people was he stricken.

9 And he made his grave with the wicked, and with the rich in his death; because he had done no violence, neither was any deceit in his mouth.

10 Yet it pleased the Lord to bruise him; he hath put him to grief: when thou shalt make his soul an offering for sin, he shall see his seed, he shall prolong his days, and the pleasure of the Lord shall prosper in his hand.

11 He shall see of the travail of his soul, and shall be satisfied: by his knowledge shall my rightous servant justify many; for he shall bear their iniquities.

12 Therefore will I divide him a portion with the great, and he shall divide the spoil with the strong; because he hath poured out his soul unto death: and he was numbered with the transgressors; and he bare the sin of many, and made intercession for the transgressors.

FORASMUCH as many have taken in hand to set forth in order a declaration of those things which are most surely believed among us,

2 Even as they delivered them unto us, which from the beginning were eyewitnesses, and ministers of the word;

3 It seemed good to me also, having had perfect understanding of all things from the very first, to write unto thee in order, most excellent The-oph'-i-lus,

4 That thou mightest know the certainty of those things, wherein thou hast been instructed.

5 THERE was in the days of Herod, the king of Judaea, a certain priest named Zach-a-ri'-as, of the course of A-bi'-a: and his wife was of the daughters of Aaron, and her name was Elisabeth.

6 And they were both righteous before God, walking in all the commandments and ordinances of the Lord blameless.

7 And they had no child, because that Elisabeth was barren, and they both were now well stricken in years.

8 And it came to pass, that while he executed the priest's office before God in the order of his course,

9 According to the custom of the priest's office, his lot was to burn incense when he went into the temple of the Lord.

10 And the whole multitude of the people were praying without at the time of incense.

11 And there appeared unto him an angel of the Lord standing on the right side of the altar of incense.

12 And when Zach-a-ri'-as saw him, he was troubled, and fear fell upon him.

13 But the angel said unto him, Fear not, Zach-a-ri'as: for thy prayer is heard; and thy wife Elisabeth shall bear thee a son, and thou shalt call his name John.

14 And thou shalt have joy and gladness; and many shall rejoice at his birth.

15 For he shall be great in the sight of the Lord, and shall drink neither wine nor strong drink; and he shall be filled with the Holy Ghost, even from his mother's womb.

16 And many of the children of Israel shall he turn to the Lord their God.

17 And he shall go before him in the spirit and power of E-li'-as, to turn the hearts of the fathers to the children, and the disobedient to the wisdom of the just; to make ready a people prepared for the Lord.

18 And Zach-a-ri'-as said unto the angel, Whereby shall I know this? for I am an old man, and my wife well stricken in years.

19 And the angel answering said unto him, I am Gabriel, that stand in the presence of God; and am sent to speak unto thee, and to shew thee these glad tidings.

20 And, behold, thou shalt be dumb, and not able to speak, until the day that these things shall be performed, because thou believest not my words, which shall be fulfilled in their season.

21 And the people waited for Zach-a-ri'-as, and marvelled that he tarried so long in the temple.

22 And when he came out, he could not speak unto them: and they perceived that he had seen a vision in the temple: for he beckoned unto them, and remained speechless.

23 And it came to pass, that, as soon as the days of his ministration were accomplished, he departed to his own house.

24 And after those days his wife Elisabeth conceived, and hid herself five months, saying,

25 Thus hath the Lord dealt with me in the days wherein he looked on me, to take away my reproach among men.

26 And in the sixth month the angel Gabriel was sent from God unto a city of Galilee, named Nazareth,

27 To a virgin espoused to a man whose name was Joseph, of the house of David; and the virgin's name was Mary.

28 And the angel came in unto her, and said,

Hail, thou that art highly favoured, the Lord is with thee: blessed art thou among women.

29 And when she saw him, she was troubled at his saying, and cast in her mind what manner of salutation this should be.

30 And the angel said unto her, Fear not, Mary: for thou hast found favour with God.

31 And, behold, thou shalt conceive in thy womb, and bring forth a son, and shalt call his name JESUS.

32 He shall be great, and shall be called the Son of the Highest: and the Lord God shall give unto him the throne of his father David:

33 And he shall reign over the house of Jacob for ever; and of his kingdom there shall be no end.

34 Then said Mary unto the angel, How shall this be, seeing I know not a man?

35 And the angel answered and said unto her, The Holy Ghost shall come upon thee, and the power of the Highest shall overshadow thee: therefore also that holy thing which shall be born of thee shall be called the Son of God.

36 And, behold, thy cousin Elisabeth, she hath also conceived a son in her old age: and this is the sixth month with her, who was called barren.

37 For with God nothing shall be impossible.

38 And Mary said, Behold the handmaid of the Lord; be it unto me according to thy word. And the angel departed from her.

39 And Mary arose in those days, and went into the hill country with haste, into a city of Judah;

40 And entered into the house of Zach-a-ri'-as, and saluted Elisabeth.

41 And it came to pass, that, when Elisabeth heard the salutation of Mary, the babe leaped in her womb; and Elisabeth was filled with the Holy Ghost:

42 And she spake out with a loud voice, and said, Blessed art thou among women, and blessed is the fruit of thy womb.

43 And whence is this to me, that the mother of my Lord should come to me?

44 For, lo, as soon as the voice of thy salutation sounded in mine ears, the babe leaped in my womb for joy.

45 And blessed is she that believed: for there shall be a performance of those things which were told her from the Lord.

46 And Mary said, My soul doth magnify the Lord,

47 And my spirit hath rejoiced in God my Saviour.

48 For he hath regarded the low estate of his handmaiden: for, behold, from henceforth all generations shall call me blessed.

49 For he that is mighty hath done to me great things; and holy is his name.

50 And his mercy is on them that fear him from generation to generation.

51 He hath shewed strength with his arm; he hath scattered the proud in the imagination of their hearts.

52 He hath put down the mighty from their seats, and exalted them of low degree.

53 He hath filled the hungry with good things; and the rich he hath sent empty away.

54 He hath holpen his servant Israel, in remembrance of his mercy;

55 As he spake to our fathers, to Abraham, and to his seed for ever.

56 And Mary abode with her about three months, and returned to her own house.

57 Now Elisabeth's full time came that she should be delivered; and she brought forth a son.

58 And her neighbors and her cousins heard how the Lord had shewed great mercy upon her; and they rejoiced with her.

59 And it came to pass, that on the eighth day they came to circumcise the child; and they called him Zach-a-ri'-as, after the name of his father.

60 And his mother answered and said, Not so; but he shall be called John.

61 And they said unto her, There is none of thy kindred that is called by this name.

62 And they made signs to his father, how he would have him called.

63 And he asked for a writing table, and wrote, saying, His name is John. And they marvelled all.

64 And his mouth was opened immediately, and his tongue loosed, and he spake, and praised God.

65 And fear came on all that dwelt round about them: and all these sayings were noised abroad throughout all the hill country of Judaea.

66 And all they that heard them laid them up in their hearts, saying, What manner of child shall this be! And the hand of the Lord was with him.

67 And his father Zach-a-ri'-as was filled with the Holy Ghost, and prophesied, saying,

68 Blessed be the Lord God of Israel; for he hath visited and redeemed his people,

69 And hath raised up an horn of salvation for us in the house of his servant David;

70 As he spake by the mouth of his holy prophets, which have been since the world began:

71 That we should be saved from our enemies, and from the hand of all that hate us;

72 To perform the mercy promised to our fathers, and to remember his holy covenant;

73 The oath which he sware to our father Abraham,

74 That he would grant unto us, that we being delivered out of the hand of our enemies might serve him without fear,

75 In holiness and righteousness before him, all the days of our life.

76 And thou, child, shalt be called the prophet of the Highest: for thou shalt go before the face of the Lord to prepare his ways;

77 To give knowledge of salvation unto his people by the remission of their sins,

78 Through the tender mercy of our God; whereby the dayspring from on high hath visited us,

79 To give light to them that sit in darkness and in the shadow of death, to guide our feet into the way of peace.

80 And the child grew, and waxed strong in spirit, and was in the deserts till the day of his shewing unto Israel.

LUKE/CHAPTER 2

AND it came to pass in those days, that there went out a decree from Caesar Augustus, that all the world should be taxed.

2 (And this taxing was first made when Cy-re'-ni-us was governor of Syria.)

3 And all went to be taxed, every one into his own city.

4 And Joseph also went up from Galilee, out of the city of Nazareth, into Judaea, unto the city of David, which is called Bethlehem; (because he was of the house and lineage of David:)

5 To be taxed with Mary his espoused wife,

being great with child.

6 And so it was, that, while they were there, the days were accomplished that she should be delivered.

7 And she brought forth her firstborn son, and wrapped him in swaddling clothes, and laid him in a manger; because there was no room for them in the inn.

8 And there were in the same country shepherds abiding in the field, keeping watch over their flock by night.

9 And, lo, the angel of the Lord came upon them, and the glory of the Lord shone round about them: and they were sore afraid.

10 And the angel said unto them, Fear not: for, behold, I bring you good tidings of great joy, which shall be to all people.

11 For unto you is born this day in the city of David a Saviour, which is Christ the Lord.

12 And this shall be a sign unto you; Ye shall find the babe wrapped in swaddling clothes, lying in a manger.

13 And suddenly there was with the angel a multitude of the heavenly host praising God, and saying,

14 Glory to God in the highest, and on earth peace, good will toward men.

15 And it came to pass, as the angels were gone away from them into heaven, the shepherds said one to another, Let us now go even unto Bethlehem, and see this thing which is come to pass, which the Lord hath made known unto us.

16 And they came with haste, and found Mary, and Joseph, and the babe lying in a manger.

17 And when they had seen it, they made known abroad the saying which was told them concerning this child.

18 And all they that heard it wondered at those things which were told them by the shepherds.

19 But Mary kept all these things, and pondered them in her heart.

20 And the shepherds returned, glorifying and praising God for all the things that they had heard and seen, as it was told unto them.

21 And when eight days were accomplished for the circumcising of the child, his name was called JESUS, which was so named of the angel before he was conceived in the womb.

22 And when the days of her purification according to the law of Moses were accomplished, they brought him to Jerusalem, to present him to the Lord;

23 (As it is written in the law of the Lord, Every male that openeth the womb shall be called holy to the Lord;)

24 And to offer a sacrifice according to that which is said in the law of the Lord, A pair of turtledoves, or two young pigeons.

25 And, behold, there was a man in Jerusalem, whose name was Simeon; and the same man was just and devout, waiting for the consolation of Israel: and the Holy Ghost was upon him.

26 And it was revealed unto him by the Holy Ghost, that he should not see death, before he had seen the Lord's Christ.

27 And he came by the Spirit into the temple: and when the parents brought in the child Jesus, to do for him after the custom of the law,

28 Then took he him up in his arms, and blessed God, and said,

29 Lord, now lettest thou thy servant depart in peace, according to thy word:

30 For mine eyes have seen thy salvation,

31 Which thou hast prepared before the face of all people;

32 A light to lighten the Gentiles, and the glory of thy people Israel.

33 And Joseph and his mother marvelled at those things which were spoken of him.

34 And Simeon blessed them, and said unto Mary his mother, Behold, this child is set for the fall and rising again of many in Israel; and for a sign which shall be spoken against;

35 (Yea, a sword shall pierce through thy own soul also,) that the thoughts of many hearts may be revealed.

36 And there was one Anna, a prophetess, the daughter of Pha-nu'-el, of the tribe of A'-ser: she was of a great age, and had lived with an husband seven years from her virginity;

37 And she was a widow of about fourscore and four years, which departed not from the temple, but served God with fastings and prayers night and day.

38 And she coming in that instant gave thanks likewise unto the Lord, and spake of him to all them that looked for redemption in Jerusalem.

39 And when they had performed all things according to the law of the Lord, they returned into Galilee, to their own city Nazareth.

40 And the child grew, and waxed strong in spirit, filled with wisdom: and the grace of God was upon him.

41 Now his parents went to Jerusalem every year at the feast of the passover.

42 And when he was twelve years old, they went up to Jerusalem after the custom of the feast.

43 And when they had fulfilled the days, as they returned, the child Jesus tarried behind in Jerusalem; and Joseph and his mother knew not of it.

44 But they, supposing him to have been in the company, went a day's journey; and they sought him among their kinsfolk and acquaintance.

45 And when they found him not, they turned back again to Jerusalem, seeking him.

46 And it came to pass, that after three days they found him in the temple, sitting in the midst of the doctors, both hearing them, and asking them questions.

47 And all that heard him were astonished at his understanding and answers.

48 And when they saw him, they were amazed: and his mother said unto him, Son, why hast thou thus dealt with us? behold, thy father and I have sought thee sorrowing.

49 And he said unto them, How is it that ye sought me? wist ye not that I must be about my Father's business?

50 And they understood not the saying which he spake unto them.

51 And he went down with them, and came to Nazareth, and was subject unto them: but his mother kept all these sayings in her heart.

52 And Jesus increased in wisdom and stature, and in favour with God and man.

MATTHEW/CHAPTER 1

THE book of the generation of Jesus Christ, the son of David, the son of Abraham.

2 Abraham begat Isaac; and Isaac begat Jacob; and Jacob begat Judas and his brethren;

3 And Judas begat Phar'-es and Zar'-a of Tha'-mar; and Phar'-es begat Es'-rom; and Es'-rom begat Ar'-am;

4 And Ar'-am begat A-min'-a-dab; and A-min'-a-dab begat Na-as'-son; and Na-as'-son begat Sal'-mon;

5 And Sal'-mon begat Bo'-oz of Ra'-chab; and Bo'-oz begat O'-bed of Ruth; and O'-bed begat Jesse;

6 And Jesse begat David the king; and David the king begat Solomon of her that had been the wife of U-ri'-as;

7 And Solomon begat Ro-bo'-am; and Ro-bo'-am begat A-bi'-a; and A-bi'-a begat A'-sa;

8 And A'-sa begat Jos'-a-phat; and Jos'-a-phat begat Joram; and Joram begat O-zi'-as;

9 And O-zi'-as begat Jo'-a-tham; and Jo'-a-tham begat A'-chaz; and A'-chaz begat Ez-e-ki'-as;

10 And Ez-e-ki'-as begat Ma-nas'-ses; and Ma-nas'-ses begat Amon; and Amon begat Jo-si'-as;

11 And Jo-si'-as begat Jech-o-ni'-as and his brethren, about the time they were carried away to Babylon:

12 And after they were brought to Babylon, Jech-o-ni'-as begat Sa-la'-thi-el; and Sa-la'-thi-el begat Zo-rob'-a-bel;

13 And Zo-rob'-a-bel begat A-bi'-ud; and A-bi'-ud begat E-li'-a-kim; and E-li'-a-kim begat A'-zor;

14 And A'-zor begat Sa'-doc; and Sa'-doc begat A'-chim; and A'-chim begat E-li'-ud;

15 And E-li'-ud begat El-e-a'-zar; and El-e-a'-zar begat Mat'-than; and Mat'-than begat Jacob;

16 And Jacob begat Joseph the husband of Mary, of whom was born Jesus, who is called Christ.

17 So all the generations from Abraham to David are fourteen generations; and from David until the carrying away into Babylon are fourteen generations; and from the carrying away into Babylon unto Christ are fourteen generations.

18 Now the birth of Jesus Christ was on this wise: When as his mother Mary was espoused to Joseph, before they came together, she was found with child of the Holy Ghost.

19 Then Joseph her husband, being a just man, and not willing to make her a publick example, was minded to put her away privily.

20 But while he thought on these things, behold, the angel of the Lord appeared unto him in a dream, saying, Joseph, thou son of David, fear not to take unto thee Mary thy wife: for that which is conceived in her is of the Holy Ghost.

21 And she shall bring forth a son, and thou shalt call his name JESUS: for he shall save his people from their sins.

22 Now all this was done, that it might be fulfilled which was spoken of the Lord by the prophet, saying,

23 Behold, a virgin shall be with child, and shall bring forth a son, and they shall call his name Em-man'-u-el, which being interpreted is, God with us.

24 Then Joseph being raised from sleep did as the angel of the Lord had bidden him, and took unto him his wife:

25 And knew her not till she had brought forth her firstborn son: and he called his name JESUS.

MATTHEW/CHAPTER 2

NOW when Jesus was born in Bethlehem of Judaea in the days of Herod the king, behold, there came wise men from the east to Jerusalem.

2 Saying, Where is he that is born King of the Jews? for we have seen his star in the east, and are come to worship him.

3 When Herod the king had heard these things, he was troubled, and all Jerusalem with him.

4 And when he had gathered all the chief priests and scribes of the people together, he demanded of them where Christ should be born.

5 And they said unto him, In Bethlehem of Judaea: for thus it is written by the prophet,

6 And thou Bethlehem, in the land of Judah, art not the least among the princes of Judah: for out of these shall come a Governor, that shall rule my people Israel.

7 Then Herod, when he had privily called the wise men, inquired of them diligently what time the star appeared.

8 And he sent them to Bethlehem, and said, Go

and search diligently for the young child; and when ye have found him, bring me word again, that I may come and worship him also.

9 When they had heard the king, they departed; and, lo, the star, which they saw in the east, went before them, till it came and stood over where the young child was.

10 When they saw the star, they rejoiced with exceeding great joy.

11 And when they were come into the house, they saw the young child with Mary his mother, and fell down, and worshipped him: and when they had opened their treasures, they presented unto him gifts; gold, and frankincense, and myrrh.

12 And being warned of God in a dream that they should not return to Herod, they departed into their own country another way.

13 And when they were departed, behold, the angel of the Lord appeareth to Joseph in a dream, saying, Arise, and take the young child and his mother, and flee into Egypt, and be thou there until I bring thee word: for Herod will seek the young child to destroy him.

14 When he arose, he took the young child and his mother by night, and departed into Egypt:

15 And was there until the death of Herod: that it might be fulfilled which was spoken of the Lord by the prophet, saying, Out of Egypt have I called my son.

16 Then Herod, when he saw that he was mocked of the wise men, was exceeding wroth, and sent forth, and slew all the children that were in Bethlehem, and in all the coasts thereof, from two

years old and under, according to the time which he had diligently inquired of the wise men.

17 Then was fulfilled that which was spoken by Jeremy the prophet, saying,

18 In Ra′-ma was there a voice heard, lamentation, and weeping, and great mourning, Rachel weeping for her children, and would not be comforted, because they are not.

19 But when Herod was dead, behold, an angel of the Lord appeareth in a dream to Joseph in Egypt,

20 Saying, Arise, and take the young child and his mother, and go into the land of Israel: for they are dead which sought the young child's life.

21 And he arose, and took the young child and his mother, and came into the land of Israel.

22 But when he heard that Ar-che-la′-us did reign in Judaea in the room of his father Herod, he was afraid to go thither: notwithstanding, being warned of God in a dream, he turned aside into the parts of Galilee:

23 And he came and dwelt in a city called Nazareth: that it might be fulfilled which was spoken by the prophets, He shall be called a Nazarene.

MATTHEW/CHAPTER 3

IN those days came John the Baptist, preaching in the wilderness of Judaea,

2 And saying, Repent ye: for the kingdom of heaven is at hand.

3 For this is he that was spoken of by the prophet E-sai′-as, saying, The voice of one crying in the wilderness, Prepare ye the way of the Lord, make his paths straight.

4 And the same John had his raiment of camel's hair, and a leathern girdle about his loins; and his meat was locusts and wild honey.

5 Then went out to him Jerusalem, and all Judaea, and all the region round about Jordan,

6 And were baptized of him in Jordan, confessing their sins.

7 But when he saw many of the Pharisees and Sad′-du-cees come to his baptism, he said unto them, O generation of vipers, who hath warned you to flee from the wrath to come?

8 Bring forth therefore fruits meet for repentance:

9 And think not to say within yourselves, We

have Abraham to our father: for I say unto you, that God is able of these stones to raise up children unto Abraham.

10 And now also the axe is laid unto the root of the trees: therefore every tree which bringeth not forth good fruit is hewn down, and cast into the fire.

11 I indeed baptize you with water unto repentance: but he that cometh after me is mightier than I, whose shoes I am not worthy to bear: he shall baptize you with the Holy Ghost, and with fire:

12 Whose fan is in his hand, and he will throughly purge his floor, and gather his wheat into the garner; but he will burn up the chaff with unquenchable fire.

13 Then cometh Jesus from Galilee to Jordan unto John, to be baptized of him.

14 But John forbad him, saying, I have need to be baptized of thee, and comest thou to me?

15 And Jesus answering said unto him, Suffer it to be so now: for thus it becometh us to fulfill all righteousness. Then he suffered him.

16 And Jesus, when he was baptized, went up straightway out of the water: and, lo, the heavens were opened unto him, and he saw the Spirit of God descending like a dove, and lighting upon him:

17 And lo a voice from heaven, saying, This is my beloved Son, in whom I am well pleased.

MATTHEW/CHAPTER 4

THEN was Jesus led up of the Spirit into the wilderness to be tempted of the devil.

2 And when he had fasted forty days and forty nights, he was afterward an hungred.

3 And when the tempter came to him, he said, If thou be the Son of God, command that these stones be made bread.

4 But he answered and said, It is written, Man shall not live by bread alone, but by every word that proceedeth out of the mouth of God.

5 Then the devil taketh him up into the holy city, and setteth him on a pinnacle of the temple,

6 And saith unto him, If thou be the Son of God, cast thyself down: for it is written, He shall give his angels charge concerning thee: and in their hands they shall bear thee up, lest at any time thou dash thy foot against a stone.

7 Jesus said unto him, It is written again, Thou shalt not tempt the Lord thy God.

8 Again, the devil taketh him up into an exceeding high mountain, and sheweth him all the kingdoms of the world, and the glory of them;

9 And saith unto him, All these things will I give thee, if thou wilt fall down and worship me.

10 Then saith Jesus unto him, Get thee hence, Satan: for it is written, Thou shalt worship the Lord thy God, and him only shalt thou serve.

11 Then the devil leaveth him, and, behold, angels came and ministered unto him.

12 Now when Jesus had heard that John was cast into prison, he departed into Galilee;

13 And leaving Nazareth, he came and dwelt in Ca-per'-na-um, which is upon the sea coast, in the borders of Za-bu'-lon and Neph'-tha-lim:

14 That it might be fulfilled which was spoken by E-sai'-as the prophet, saying,

15 The land of Za-bu'-lon, and the land of Neph'-tha-lim, by the way of the sea, beyond Jordan, Galilee of the Gentiles;

16 The people which sat in darkness saw great light; and to them which sat in the region and shadow of death light is sprung up.

17 From that time Jesus began to preach, and to say, Repent: for the kingdom of heaven is at hand.

18 And Jesus, walking by the sea of Galilee, saw two brethren, Simon called Peter, and Andrew his brother, casting a net into the sea: for they were fishers.

19 And he saith unto them, Follow me, and I will make you fishers of men.

20 And they straightway left their nets, and followed him.

21 And going on from thence, he saw other two brethren, James the son of Zeb'-e-dee, and John his brother in a ship with Zeb'-e-dee their father, mending their nets; and he called them.

22 And they immediately left the ship and their father, and followed him.

23 And Jesus went about all Galilee, teaching in their synagogues, and preaching the gospel of the kingdom, and healing all manner of sickness and all manner of disease among the people.

24 And his fame went throughout all Syria: and they brought unto him all sick people that were taken with divers diseases and torments, and those which were possessed with devils, and those which were lunatick, and those that had the palsy; and he healed them.

25 And there followed him great multitudes of people from Galilee, and from De-cap'-o-lis, and from Jerusalem, and from Judaea, and from beyond Jordan.

MATTHEW/CHAPTER 5

AND seeing the multitudes, he went up into a mountain: and when he was set, his disciples came unto him:

2 And he opened his mouth, and taught them, saying,

3 Blessed are the poor in spirit: for theirs is the kingdom of heaven.

4 Blessed are they that mourn: for they shall be comforted.

5 Blessed are the meek: for they shall inherit the earth.

6 Blessed are they which do hunger and thirst after righteousness: for they shall be filled.

7 Blessed are the merciful: for they shall obtain mercy.

8 Blessed are the pure in heart: for they shall see God.

9 Blessed are the peacemakers: for they shall be called the children of God.

10 Blessed are they which are persecuted for righteousness' sake: for theirs is the kingdom of heaven.

11 Blessed are ye, when men shall revile you, and persecute you, and shall say all manner of evil against you falsely, for my sake.

12 Rejoice, and be exceeding glad: for great is your reward in heaven: for so persecuted they the prophets which were before you.

13 Ye are the salt of the earth: but if the salt have lost his savour, wherewith shall it be salted? it is thenceforth good for nothing, but to be cast out, and to be trodden under foot of men.

14 Ye are the light of the world. A city that is set on an hill cannot be hid.

15 Neither do men light a candle, and put it under a bushel, but on a candlestick; and it giveth light unto all that are in the house.

16 Let your light so shine before men, that they may see your good works, and glorify your Father which is in heaven.

17 Think not that I am come to destroy the law, or the prophets: I am not come to destroy, but to fulfill.

18 For verily I say unto you, Till heaven and earth pass, one jot or one tittle shall in no wise pass from the law, till all be fulfilled.

19 Whosoever therefore shall break one of these least commandments, and shall teach men so, he shall be called the least in the kingdom of heaven: but whosoever shall do and teach them, the same shall be called great in the kingdom of heaven.

20 For I say unto you, That except your righteousness shall exceed the righteousness of the

scribes and Pharisees, ye shall in no case enter into the kingdom of heaven.

21 Ye have heard that it was said by them of old time, Thou shalt not kill; and whosoever shall kill shall be in danger of the judgment:

22 But I say unto you, That whosoever is angry with his brother without a cause shall be in danger of the judgment: and whosoever shall say to his brother, Ra'-ca, shall be in danger of the council: but whosoever shall say, Thou fool, shall be in danger of hell fire.

23 Therefore if thou bring thy gift to the altar, and there rememberest that thy brother hath aught against thee;

24 Leave there thy gift before the altar, and go thy way; first be reconciled to thy brother, and then come and offer thy gift.

25 Agree with thine adversary quickly, whiles thou art in the way with him; lest at any time the adversary deliver thee to the judge, and the judge deliver thee to the officer, and thou be cast into prison.

26 Verily I say unto thee, Thou shalt by no means come out thence, till thou hast paid the uttermost farthing.

27 Ye have heard that it was said by them of old time, Thou shalt not commit adultery:

28 But I say unto you, That whosoever looketh on a woman to lust after her hath committed adultery with her already in his heart.

29 And if thy right eye offend thee, pluck it out, and cast it from thee: for it is profitable for thee that one of thy members should perish, and not that thy whole body should be cast into hell.

30 And if thy right hand offend thee, cut it off, and cast it from thee: for it is profitable for thee that one of thy members should perish, and not that thy whole body should be cast into hell.

31 It hath been said, Whosoever shall put away his wife, let him give her a writing of divorcement:

32 But I say unto you, That whosoever shall put away his wife, saving for the cause of fornication, causeth her to commit adultery: and whosoever shall marry her that is divorced committeth adultery.

33 Again, ye have heard that it hath been said by them of old time, Thou shalt not forswear thyself, but shalt perform unto the Lord thine oaths:

34 But I say unto you, Swear not at all; neither

by heaven; for it is God's throne:

35 Nor by the earth; for it is his footstool: neither by Jerusalem; for it is the city of the great King.

36 Neither shalt thou swear by thy head, because thou canst not make one hair white or black.

37 But let your communication be, Yea, yea; Nay, nay: for whatsoever is more than these cometh of evil.

38 Ye have heard that it hath been said, An eye for an eye, and a tooth for a tooth:

39 But I say unto you, That ye resist not evil: but whosoever shall smite thee on thy right cheek, turn to him the other also.

40 And if any man will sue thee at the law, and take away thy coat, let him have thy cloak also.

41 And whosoever shall compel thee to go a mile, go with him twain.

42 Give to him that asketh thee, and from him that would borrow of thee turn not thou away.

43 Ye have heard that it hath been said, Thou shalt love thy neighbour, and hate thine enemy.

44 But I say unto you, Love your enemies, bless them that curse you, do good to them that hate you, and pray for them which despitefully use you, and persecute you;

45 That ye may be the children of your Father which is in heaven: for he maketh his sun to rise on the evil and on the good, and sendeth rain on the just and on the unjust.

46 For if ye love them which love you, what reward have ye? do not even the publicans the same?

47 And if ye salute your brethren only, what do ye more than others? do not even the publicans so?

48 Be ye therefore perfect, even as your Father which is in heaven is perfect.

MATTHEW/CHAPTER 6

TAKE heed that ye do not your alms before men, to be seen of them: otherwise ye have no reward of your father which is in heaven.

2 Therefore when thou doest thine alms, do not sound a trumpet before thee, as the hypocrites do in the synagogues and in the streets, that they may have glory of men. Verily I say unto you, They have their reward.

3 But when thou doest alms, let not thy left

hand know what thy right hand doeth:

4 That thine alms may be in secret: and thy Father which seeth in secret himself shall reward thee openly.

5 And when thou prayest, thou shalt not be as the hypocrites are: for they love to pray standing in the synagogues and in the corners of the streets, that they may be seen of men. Verily I say unto you, They have their reward.

6 But thou, when thou prayest, enter into thy closet, and when thou has shut thy door, pray to thy Father which is in secret; and thy Father which seeth in secret shall reward thee openly.

7 But when ye pray, use not vain repetitions, as the heathen do: for they think that they shall be heard for their much speaking.

8 Be not ye therefore like unto them: for your Father knoweth what things ye have need of, before ye ask him.

9 After this manner therefore pray ye: Our Father which art in heaven, Hallowed be thy name.

10 Thy kingdom come. Thy will be done in earth, as it is in heaven.

11 Give us this day our daily bread.

12 And forgive us our debts, as we forgive our debtors.

13 And lead us not into temptation, but deliver us from evil: For thine is the kingdom, and the power, and the glory, for ever. A'-men.

14 For if ye forgive men their trespasses, your heavenly Father will also forgive you:

15 But if ye forgive not men their trespasses, neither will your Father forgive your trespasses.

16 Moreover when ye fast, be not, as the hypocrites, of a sad countenance: for they disfigure their faces, that they may appear unto men to fast. Verily I say unto you, They have their reward.

17 But thou, when thou fastest, anoint thine head, and wash thy face;

18 That thou appear not unto men to fast, but unto thy Father which is in secret: and thy Father, which seeth in secret, shall reward thee openly.

19 Lay not up for yourselves treasures upon earth, where moth and rust doth corrupt, and where thieves break through and steal:

20 But lay up for yourselves treasures in heaven, where neither moth nor rust doth corrupt, and where thieves do not break through nor steal:

21 For where your treasure is, there will your heart be also.

22 The light of the body is the eye: if therefore thine eye be single, thy whole body shall be full of light.

23 But if thine eye be evil, thy whole body shall be full of darkness. If therefore the light that is in thee be darkness, how great is that darkness!

24 No man can serve two masters: for either he will hate the one, and love the other; or else he will hold to the one, and despise the other. Ye cannot serve God and mammon.

25 Therefore I say unto you, Take no thought for your life, what ye shall eat, or what ye shall drink; nor yet for your body, what ye shall put on. Is not the life more than meat, and the body than raiment?

26 Behold the fowls of the air: for they sow not, neither do they reap, nor gather into barns; yet your heavenly Father feedeth them. Are ye not much better than they?

27 Which of you by taking thought can add one cubit unto his stature?

28 And why take ye thought for raiment? Consider the lilies of the field, how they grow; they toil not, neither do they spin:

29 And yet I say unto you, That even Solomon in all his glory was not arrayed like one of these.

30 Wherefore, if God so clothe the grass of the field, which today is, and tomorrow is cast into the

oven, shall he not much more clothe you, O ye of little faith?

31 Therefore take no thought, saying, What shall we eat? or, What shall we drink? or, Wherewithal shall we be clothed?

32 (For after all these things do the Gentiles seek:) for your heavenly Father knoweth that ye have need of all these things.

33 But seek ye first the kingdom of God, and his righteousness; and all these things shall be added unto you.

34 Take therefore no thought for the morrow: for the morrow shall take thought for the things of itself. Sufficient unto the day is the evil thereof.

MATTHEW/CHAPTER 7

JUDGE not, that ye be not judged.

2 For with what judgment ye judge, ye shall be judged: and with what measure ye mete, it shall be measured to you again.

3 And why beholdest thou the mote that is in thy brother's eye, but considerest not the beam that is in thine own eye?

4 Or how wilt thou say to thy brother, Let me pull out the mote out of thine eye; and, behold, a beam is in thine own eye?

5 Thou hypocrite, first cast out the beam out of thine own eye; and then shalt thou see clearly to cast out the mote out of thy brother's eye.

6 Give not that which is holy unto the dogs, neither cast ye your pearls before swine, lest they trample them under their feet, and turn again and rend you.

7 Ask, and it shall be given you; seek, and ye shall find; knock, and it shall be opened unto you:

8 For every one that asketh receiveth; and he that seeketh findeth; and to him that knocketh it shall be opened.

9 Or what man is there of you, whom if his son ask bread, will he give him a stone?

10 Or if he ask a fish, will he give him a serpent?

11 If ye then, being evil, know how to give good gifts unto your children, how much more shall your Father which is in heaven give good things to them that ask him?

12 Therefore all things whatsoever ye would that men should do to you, do ye even so to them:

for this is the law and the prophets.

13 Enter ye in at the strait gate: for wide is the gate, and broad is the way, that leadeth to destruction, and many there be which go in thereat:

14 Because strait is the gate, and narrow is the way, which leadeth unto life, and few there be that find it.

15 Beware of false prophets, which come to you in sheep's clothing, but inwardly they are ravening wolves.

16 Ye shall know them by their fruits. Do men gather grapes of thorns, or figs of thistles?

17 Even so every good tree bringeth forth good fruit; but a corrupt tree bringeth forth evil fruit.

18 A good tree cannot bring forth evil fruit, neither can a corrupt tree bring forth good fruit.

19 Every tree that bringeth not forth good fruit is hewn down, and cast into the fire.

20 Wherefore by their fruits ye shall know them.

21 Not every one that saith unto me, Lord, Lord, shall enter into the kingdom of heaven; but he that doeth the will of my Father which is in heaven.

22 Many will say to me in that day, Lord, Lord, have we not prophesied in thy name? and in thy name have cast out devils? and in thy name done many wonderful works?

23 And then will I profess unto them, I never knew you: depart from me, ye that work iniquity.

24 Therefore whosoever heareth these sayings of mine, and doeth them, I will liken him unto a wise man, which built his house upon a rock:

25 And the rain descended, and the floods came, and the winds blew, and beat upon that house; and it fell not: for it was founded upon a rock.

26 And every one that heareth these sayings of mine, and doeth them not, shall be likened unto a foolish man, which built his house upon the sand:

27 And the rain descended, and the floods came, and the winds blew, and beat upon that house; and it fell: and great was the fall of it.

28 And it came to pass, when Jesus had ended these sayings, the people were astonished at his doctrine:

29 For he taught them as one having authority, and not as the scribes.

■ ■ ■

IERUSALEM

A Psephina tower
B Womens tower
C Herods Pallace
D Hipius tower
E Gate Ephraim
F Gate Benjamin
G Assirian castell
H Water Gate
I Dunghill Gate
K Sheps Gate
L Sheps Poole
M Monobaz Pallace
N Ezekias Poole
O Antonius Pallace
P Paved Street
Q Agrippas Pallace
R Essens Gate
S Old Gate
T Salomons Pallace
V Shiloe Gate
W Fountains of Shiloe
X Bathing Poole
Y Salomons Garden
Z Fish-Poole
1 Goulden Gate
2 Fish Gate
3 Upper mont
4 Lower mont
5 Hananael tower
6 Josaphats sepul.
7 Isays sepulchre
8 Davids sepulchre
9 Davids tower
10 Arc in Sion
11 Millo

Kedron flu

M. Olivet.

Valei Hinn.

With our shedding of bloud is no remisssion Heb 9. 22.

MIDDLE

SEA

THE ÆGYPTIAN SEA

DATMETICUM TANISTIUM TANITICUM PELUSIACUM

Damiata
Garenorium

Sirbons Lac.

RIVER OF EGIPT or

PALUDES Hercules parua KENITES Sabes
Wildernes of Iurie

MENDESIÆ NOM.

Daphne Pelusie

Phatuna

SETHROITES NOM.

GESHURITS & GERZITES

NEUTIS NOM.

ONUPHITES NOM.

BUBASTI NOM.

Bubassus

THE WILDERNES OF SHUR

WILDERNES OF PARAN

Kadesh Barnea

Kadesh

BUSIRITES NOM.

PHERBET NOM.

Paran

Graves of Lust

BUBASTICUS FLU.

Seraphuum

ÆGYPT

Pharbetus

Mont Sinai

WILDERNES OF ZIN

Midian

Rephidim OF SINAI

Aluss

LAND OF GOSHEN

Dophkah OF ZIN

COUNTRIE OF NEBAIOTH

Ramases

Succoth

Etham

WILDERNES

Zin

Nebaioth

Chethia

Etham

TRAIANUS RIVER HERDOPOLITE.

Iam Suph

Elim

Marah

Naphtali

Iudah

Magdol

Marah

Dan

Benjamin

Manasses

Simeon

COUNTRIE OF KEDAR

Ephraim

PTOLOMEUS RIVER

Gad

Koahitis

Reuben

Zebulon

Cleopatrida

RED SEA OR ARABIAN

THE SCALE OF MILES

And the Lord spake unto Moses, saying: "Behold, the land of Canaan." (Deuteronomy, 32, 48)

In the time of Christ, the land of Canaan was comprised of Judaea (IU-DE-A) in the south, Samaria (SA-MA-RIA) to the north and Galilee (GAL-LI-LE) in the far north. Today, Israel and Jordan occupy the territories of Judaea and Samaria, while Lebanon and part of Syria cover the area once known as Galilee. Egypt lies to the southwest, with (Saudi) Arabia to the southeast.

This annotated map, with a detail of the city of Jerusalem (upper left) appeared in the first edition of the King James Bible, published in 1611.

The legend to the right includes references to Bethlehem (in the center, southwest of Jerusalem), where "Christ ye glorie of Ifraell and light of ye gentills was born" (34); and the place by the River Jordan, flowing north from the Dead sea, "wherein John did baptize" Christ (23); Finally, "all ye townes & places which ye Scriptures nameth in them are exactlie sett downe . . . all tending to make more plane unto us the histories of the holie Scripture, both in ould and newe testament . ."

MADONNA AND CHILD
*A crayon drawing by
Raphael (1483-1520)*

THE ARTISTS

Who are these artists and what made them paint the Christian story as they did?

Saint or scientist, historian or poet, sycophant or satirist, chronicler or prophet—each belonged to his own country and tradition, expressing the spirit of his time.

Medieval painting was not the portrayal of things seen, but the presentation of beliefs. In the Middle Ages, the real world was an insignificant dream—a mere prelude to an afterlife of perfect joy or terror. Thus artists were indifferent to the natural world and painted pictures of heaven or hell, not of earth. Their stiff, immobile figures against gold backgrounds are symbols for contemplation, abstract representations of the ideas of the Church.

Slowly, the fear which had gripped the Christian world gave way to a more human and joyful faith, inspiring a new naturalism. Saint Francis left the darkness of the monastery to preach under an open sky—and the artists followed him. They looked at the world and everywhere they saw visible signs of God. Every tree, every plant and stone became a tangible proof of God's existence. At first, the painters' attempts to portray the figure of Christ in a natural landscape were stumbling and their technique was primitive. Then, in Flanders, Gerard David and Memling, heirs to a greater skill in drawing the smallest details of nature, made the message of the Church more alive and compelling. The doves in David's *Baptism of Christ* and *Annunciation* symbolize the Holy Ghost, but they bear an increasing resemblance to real birds in flight.

While the Flemish painters were applying a magnifying glass to nature, the Italians were creating ideal forms based on reality. In Renaissance Florence, where man had become the measure of all things and the center of a rationally conceived world, Masaccio painted Christ as the ideal man, proud and self-confident, standing firmly on the earth. Giorgione, responding to a more humanized and personal feeling, presented the Madonna as a gentle Venetian matron reading to the Christ Child in her own home. This combination of representation and idealism reached its peak in Raphael's balanced forms, and remained suspended there—but not for long. Already there were forces at work urging a greater emotional involvement, increased and more direct personal expression. In the Raphael drawing (opposite), the Madonna begins to move; she turns and seems ready to speak. A new way of looking at the Christian story was forming in men's minds.

When Raphael died in 1520 the tide of the Reformation had begun to sweep across Northern Europe. Protestants denounced images as idolatrous, and rejected them in favor of the spoken and printed word. The Bible was translated; copies came from the newly invented printing press and for the first time became easily accessible to the common man. Rembrandt, reading his Bible closely, depicted scenes from the New Testament never presented before. He showed Christ as a teacher, illustrated His words, and painted His portrait with deep psychological insight. But Protestantism neither patronized nor encouraged religious painting.

Northern European artists flocked to Italy, where the Counter-Reformation was in progress. At the Council of Trent (1545-63), painters were urged not to abandon religious images, but to dramatize them, to make them more real than ever. In an age essentially preoccupied with materialism, the Church encouraged artists to appeal to men's emotions and their senses. Rubens painted powerful, muscular figures, larger than life—not mystical, but tangible and voluptuous. This trend toward the dramatic characterized the Baroque style of the seventeenth century. But Rubens was the last to depict a world both divine and human. After him, the focus of painting turned increasingly to the real world. Lorrain's *Sermon on the Mount* reveals a Romantic delight in the beauties of nature, in which Christ and His Disciples are less prominent than the natural world around them.

Each artist individually mirrors the world which created him. The sum of their lives holds a key to the historical evolution of the Christian story in art.

Andrea di Giusto ?-1455 • FLORENTINE

CHRIST AND APOSTLES IN A TEM-PLE, *John G. Johnson Collection, Philadelphia, page* 91.

Born in Florence in the early years of the fifteenth century, Andrea di Giusto lived in one of the most exciting artistic environments the world has ever known. Yet he was himself torn between two conflicting styles, caught in the uncertainty between the distintegration of the Medieval world and the emerging Renaissance.

It was Andrea's plight to have come under the influence of the leading exponents of each school: Lorenzo Monaco and Masaccio. He began as a pupil and follower of Lorenzo, from whom he learned to paint in the elegant and decorative Gothic style, less concerned with the imitation of nature than with the symbolic presentation of the moral and religious lessons of the Church. Then, in 1426, he was suddenly exposed to all the force of the new realism in the person of the young Masaccio, with whom he worked as an assistant in Pisa. The effect on Andrea was immediate and pronounced, but not decisive. Fascinated by the new technique of representing space and depth by means of perspective, he still could not shake off the old Gothic forms. In 1436, ten years after his Pisan experience, he painted an altarpiece which is a faithful copy of one done by Lorenzo thirty years before, marking his total reversion to the conservative style.

In the painting *Christ and Apostles in a Temple,* the mingling of old and new can be seen. The figures stand in a Renaissance building whose exaggerated perspective dominates the painting. Yet the whole concept is still Medieval, with its episodic narrative, stiff and impersonal figures, and decorative use of line and color.

Giovanni Bellini c. 1430-1516 • VENETIAN

FLIGHT INTO EGYPT, *(detail), National Gallery, Washington,* pages 44-45.

Giovanni Bellini, the greatest of a family of three great painters, played a vital part in the transformation of painting which occurred in Venice in the fifteenth century. His father Jacopo, born in 1400, was rooted in the Gothic tradition, but by the time of Giovanni's death in 1516 the lives of father and son had spanned that momentous rebirth of art and learning in Italy called the Renaissance.

Giovanni was born in Venice about 1430, a year or two after his brother Gentile. The two boys received their first training at their father's workshop, helping him with large historical paintings as well as the processional banners and other decorations which then constituted a large part of an artist's commissions. These processions and pageants, with the Doge and Senators dressed in splendid costumes, winding through the fairy-tale city of canals and gilded palaces, were an important visual and emotional part of Venetian life. Their color and sense of spectacle dazzled and inspired the painter's eye. Much of Venetian painting, including works of both Jacopo and Gentile, resemble or recall these colorful and solemn pageants, and in many cases actually represent them. But in the work of the young Giovanni there appear qualities new to Venetian painting, an increased involvement in the technical problems of representing reality and a deeper spiritual content.

Giovanni, more than his elder brother, was by temperament suited to respond to the new spirit in painting which was forming in Northern Italy in the early years of the fifteenth century. It was a time of great ferment and growth: artists, inspired by the revival of classical learning and the growing importance of the individual, had turned their eyes from heaven down to earth. Man was the center of the world and suddenly the object of endless curiosity and delight. Now the talents of the young painters and sculptors were turned to an examination of man in this world and to discovering the means of representing both man and nature through anatomy, perspective, and the rendering of forms in light and space. One of the outstanding figures in this scientific analysis of the visible world was the young Paduan, Andrea Mantegna, about five years older than Giovanni and a brilliant draftsman and anatomist. He married Giovanni's older sister Nicolosia and remained in close contact with the young Venetian, exercising a profound influence on his development and understanding of the new means of expression.

Except for some time in Padua, Giovanni spent his life in Venice. He maintained a workshop with his brother and, in 1479, when Gentile left for Constantinople to paint the Sultan's portrait, Giovanni assumed the care of paintings in the Doge's palace, a position of considerable prestige. From this time on his name appears frequently in the city records and he executed many commissions both public and private, for frescoes and single paintings on canvas. In 1483 he was appointed official painter to the Republic of Venice, the highest honor that city could offer, and was thereby exempted from all obligations to the Guild of Painters. He had become a standard and measure unto himself.

In his later years he retained this position and was extremely influential among the younger painters, including both Titian and Giorgione, his pupils. More than any other single painter, he determined the direction taken by Venetian painting in the period of its great flowering—the late fifteenth, and sixteenth centuries.

The Venetians, primarily visual painters fascinated by the changing aspects of the world, were less theoretical than the Florentines, intent on discovering the laws which underlie appearances. The Venetians were, above all, painters of light and color; and Bellini was especially sensitive to variations of natural light and effects of atmosphere. One of the first to adopt the Flemish technique of glazing in oil over tempera, he used it to give luminosity and vibrancy to both figures and landscapes. His *Flight into Egypt* is a lyrical celebration of the beauty of nature and of man's harmony with the world in which he lives.

Pietro Bellotti 1625-1700 • ITALIAN

Pietro Bellotti gained a reputation in his day principally for his portraits. Among his influential patrons were two cardinals—one of whom later became Pope Alexander III. Bellotti was commissioned by Maximilian II of Bavaria to paint his wife, the Princess Henriette-Adelaide, and the painter reputedly enjoyed an "affaire du coeur" with the Princess.

He was born at Bolzano, spent the majority of his working years in the northern part of Italy, and died at Lake Garda near his birthplace. The cities which he is known to have visited form a triangle across the top of the country: Mantua, Milan and Monaco. An extension of the eastern side of the triangle points directly to Venice, and his style owes much to Venetian painting. His courtly figures with mannered gestures, set in grandiose backgrounds, suggest Veronese and Titian, while his idealized faces of sweetness and tranquility recall the earlier Venetian master, Bellini.

In *Christ Disputing with the Elders,* the artist probably modeled the faces of the Elders on Venetian noblemen of the day. These proud, dogmatic, aristocratic types contrast with the pure and innocent face of Jesus, drawn after the Classical ideal which had dominated the Renaissance. Conversely, the isolation of the pointing hands and theatrical use of light to illumine the open books signal the deliberate policy of the Church, during the Counter-Reformation, to encourage artists to popularize and dramatize the Scriptures.

CHRIST DISPUTING THE ELDERS, (detail),Bob Jones University, Greenville, South Carolina, pages 70-71.

Carl Heinrich Bloch 1834-1890 • DANISH

Carl Bloch entered a school for Marine cadets at the age of fifteen, but renounced this career to become a student in the Fine Arts. After winning the distinguished Prix de Rome, he moved from Denmark to Italy and remained there until 1865. Upon his return to Denmark, he was made a member of the Academy of Copenhagen, later becoming a professor at the School of Fine Arts. At the Exposition of 1878, he received the Legion of Honor decoration.

The painter's popular and sentimental religious art is characteristic of the representative school of painting of the nineteenth century. Bloch's particular quality is his curious pastel-like coloring, and flair for dramatizing the events of Christ's life with a twentieth-century motion picture-like realism and spontaneity.

The quantity of work produced by Bloch is matched only by the range of his subject matter. Today, the permanent collections of many museums contain such disparate works as: *Samson in the Mill, Table in the Kitchen, Christian II in the Prison of Sonderburg, Woman Asleep* and *Young Girl Inhaling a Rose.*

SERMON ON THE MOUNT, (detail), Frederiksborg Castle, Hillerod, Denmark, pages 126-127.

Francesco Botticini 1446-1497 · FLORENTINE

MADONNA, *(detail), The Louvre, Paris, pages* **34-35.**

The names of the painters with whom Botticini studied or worked, or whose manner he adopted, read like a catalogue of the finest artists of his day: Verrocchio, Botticelli, Filippino Lippi, Castagno, Cosimo Rosselli, Domenico Ghirlandaio, and Pollaiuolo. It is a formidable list of styles to have molded the work of any young painter. Consequently, it is not surprising that the pictures ascribed to Botticini are diverse in both form and content. According to contemporary accounts, he tried his hand at imitating, in turn, most of the prominent painters of his time.

At the age of thirteen, he was apprenticed to the painter Neri di Bicci, who headed a large and busy workshop in Florence. In fifteenth-century Italy, painters were craftsmen equal in status to the other tradesmen of the city—butchers, clock makers and apothecaries. Each master painter took a number of boys as apprentices who received no pay—only food, shelter, clothing and instruction. This was not an easy life: their daily routine was made up of such menial tasks as grinding pigments, preparing media and panels and cleaning the shop. Only after a number of years did they receive instruction in drawing and painting. The apprentice was bound to the master for a period of five to ten years, after which he became a paid assistant or, if talented enough, a master on his own.

Even at thirteen Botticini seems to have been rebellious and inconstant. He ran away from di Bicci after only nine months and it is not known where he completed his apprenticeship. Perhaps he studied with the great painter and sculptor Verrocchio, or possibly with a number of different masters.

Botticini's work is closer in style to the gentle, lyrical feeling of Botticelli and Fra Filippo Lippi than to the vigorous, scientific approach of Masaccio, Mantegna and Paolo Uccello. The girlish face of Botticini's *Madonna* provides a striking contrast to the mature somewhat sedate models often chosen by other artists to depict the Virgin. Behind her a soft, idyllic landscape unfolds, its quiet winding stream and delicate trees reflecting the Madonna's mood of peace and harmony.

Like Botticelli, Botticini came into conflict with the moral authority of the Church. His *Assumption of the Virgin* was declared by the ecclesiastical powers to contain certain heresies, and to prevent the corruption of the faithful, they ordered the painting covered near the end of the fifteenth century. Such cases were rare in the early Renaissance, for it was not until after the Reformation and the Council of Trent that the Church began to exercise stricter control over the wayward individualism of the Renaissance humanists.

Jean Bourdichon 1457-1521 · FRENCH

ANNUNCIATION TO THE SHEP-HERDS, *miniature, (detail), Bibliothèque Nationale, Paris,* pages **28-29.**

The only factual traces of Jean Bourdichon's life which exist today are in obscure, forgotten court registers and receipts from the French royal treasuries. Yet in his lifetime he was one of the most celebrated court painters, employed by four different kings of France: Louis XI, Charles VIII, Louis XII and Francis I. Most of his portraits and paintings have disappeared, with the exception of a triptych at Naples and a portrait of Anne of Brittany. Typical of all Medieval artists, Bourdichon was a versatile craftsman at the service of his patrons. He designed coins, lamps, and reliquaries; painted portraits, landscapes, and banners; and illuminated prayer books and manuscripts. Louis XI commissioned him to decorate the Royal Chapel at Pléssis-les-Tours in 1478, and from 1484 on he bore the title 'Painter of the King.'

Five surviving illuminated manuscripts can be tentatively attributed to him, but only one, a Book of Hours (an illustrated prayer book) is definitely by his hand. The *Annunciation to the Shepherds* is a miniature painting from one of these manuscripts. Bourdichon sets the scene in a meadow near a Medieval castle of ramparts and towers. The shepherds, simple and stocky French peasants, receive the angel's message with wonder and awe, one of them raising his hand to shield his eyes from the dazzling light. Every detail is drawn with painstaking exactness, and the light which showers on them reflects from every surface and fold.

The last of the great French miniaturists, Bourdichon still belonged in spirit to the waning Middle Ages, yet his work shows signs of the gathering Renaissance. His meticulous realism, so characteristic of the late Medieval mind, is unified by the enveloping light, relating man to nature in a harmonious whole. From such miniatures as these grew the art of landscape painting in Northern Europe.

Dirk Bouts c. 1415-1475 • FLEMISH

Dirk Bouts was born a Dutchman and grew up in the flat farm country of northern Holland. It is not certain with whom, or even where, Bouts served his apprenticeship—but he probably studied first in his native Haarlem. It is also possible he worked at Brussels, where he would have come under the powerful influence of Rogier van der Weyden. He was certainly indebted to Rogier, especially in his understanding of psychological content and emotional expression. The styles of the two men are so similar, in fact, that some historians think Bouts may have been Rogier's pupil.

He was about thirty when he arrived in Louvain, a city then bursting with artistic activity. He married the daughter of a prominent burgher soon after his arrival, and it was a fortunate match for the talented young painter. Bouts was now brought into close contact with the wealthy middle class who were becoming increasingly active as patrons of the arts. It is not certain whether he remained in Louvain or returned for a short time to Haarlem, but the city records establish his presence at Louvain in 1457, where he spent the rest of his life. Apparently a painter of considerable rank, he was given large commissions by the city and local confraternities, taking part in the decorations for the great festivals and processions which occurred when persons of high rank visited the city.

In 1464 he received an important commission for an altarpiece depicting the Last Supper and related scenes from the Old Testament, which occupied him for four years. Bouts was appointed official Town Painter while working on it, a distinction which carried with it both increased prestige and a number of side benefits. Every year he received from the city a robe and a sum of money for a coat lining as an official bonus. He also had the privilege and obligation of marching in the annual procession of the Holy Sacrament, being compensated for this exhausting march by an allotment of Rhine wine.

After the death of his first wife in 1473, Bouts married again; but he lived only two more years, dying on May 6, 1475. At the time of his death he was working on a sequence of four pictures called "Examples of Justice"—illustrations of the gruesome punishments inflicted on unjust magistrates. These were to hang in the new town hall, to inspire the judges with due respect for their civil and moral responsibilities. Only two of the panels were partially completed before he died. The Burgomaster, no doubt intent on avoiding the danger of an unjust settlement, called another painter to decide their value and paid more than half the promised sum to Bouts' widow.

The technical virtuosity of the Flemish artists in the depiction of surface reality takes on a new meaning in Bouts' work. He renders every contour of face and hands with the greatest care and patience, lingering over the outlines of each form. Yet this description of outward appearances is transformed by Bouts' personal sensibility into a poignant penetration of the mystery of human personality. Remote and intense, his figures exist in a world of heightened awareness where emotion is held and transfigured—suspended in time.

Robert Campin c. 1379-1444 • FLEMISH

The mystery which envelops the identity of this painter is typical of the veil of anonymity which hides many as yet nameless early Flemish painters. Many paintings exist whose authors are unknown, since the signing of works had not yet become customary. In the archives of the various cities the names of scores of painters are recorded to whom no known works can be attributed. To search out the infrequent and often ambiguous clues and, like a detective, match painter to paintings remains a challenge.

For many years a number of unidentified works were grouped together because of similarities in style and their unknown painter was called by the following curious names: The Master of the Mousetrap, from a detail in the *Triptych of the Annunciation;* The Master of

VIRGIN AND CHILD, *(detail),* *Metropolitan Museum of Art, New York, page* **54.**

CHRIST APPROACHING THE HOUSE OF MARY AND MARTHA, *(detail), The National Trust (Upton House), England, pages* **88-89.**

THE ENTOMBMENT, *(detail of mourning figures), National Gallery, London, pages* **130-131.**

CAMPIN ALTARPIECE: TRIPTYCH OF THE ANNUNCIATION, *(right wing), Joseph as a Carpenter, Metropolitan Museum of Art, The Cloisters, New York, page* **55.**

HEAD OF CHRIST AND THE VIRGIN, *(detail), John G. Johnson Collection, Philadelphia, pages* **84-85.**

Mérode, from the name of a former owner of this painting; and most obscurely of all, as The Master of Flémalle, from the location of a hypothetical abbey where a number of the paintings are supposed to have been found. Many of them had been considered youthful works of the great Rogier van der Weyden. Then, when it was discovered that Rogier's unknown teacher was Robert Campin, the mystery was solved.

Campin is first heard of as a master painter working in Tournai in 1406. Four years later he became a citizen of that town, indicating that he had been born elsewhere, probably at Valenciennes sometime between 1375 and 1380. In Tournai he successfully maintained a large workshop which never lacked commissions nor apprentices to carry them out. Campin was drawn into politics in 1423 by a revolt of the organized craftsmen of Tournai against the city government, and in the same year was appointed Dean of the Painters Guild. This threw him into the center of the new government and he was a member of the de facto city council until 1428, when the middle class regained control. He then attempted to retire from public life, but without success, for he was accused of what would today be called 'un-Tournaisian activities' and, as one historian puts it, "mildly persecuted." He was also reprimanded by the new City Fathers for certain irregularities in his private life—'living in concubinage'—for which he was ordered to make a pilgrimage to Provence, during one year's banishment. This sentence was reduced by the intervention of the reigning princess, to the payment of a fine. None of this seriously interfered with his career, and he continued to live and work in Louvain, receiving commissions not only from private individuals but from the city government itself. He died at Louvain in 1444.

One of the most important figures in the Flemish school, Campin is considered one of its founders, together with Jan van Eyck. His work marks the change from the lingering primitivism of the earlier miniature painting, with its naïvely naturalistic drawing and flat space, to the fully developed naturalism of the fifteenth century. This transition is seen in the rendering of the scene of Joseph practicing his trade as a carpenter in the *Campin Altarpiece*. Joseph's shop is drawn in perspective—not yet scientifically correct, but intended to create the illusion of a real space. The walls form a box with one side removed, and all the surfaces tilt forward to reveal each object and detail, drawn with the utmost care and feeling: the tools, the surface of the wood, even the stains of rust on the lifted window shutters. Nothing is too slight to escape the painter's attention. Many of these simple objects have a hidden religious significance—even the mousetrap which Joseph has just completed and set on the window ledge. This has been identified as an allusion to St. Augustine's doctrine that the marriage of the Virgin and the Incarnation of Christ were devised by Providence in order to ensnare the devil, as mice are trapped by bait. The rendering of objects was not merely an end in itself; it was the result of a spiritual need to crystallize all thought into images, to express abstract truths in concrete terms. The spirit and faith of the Middle Ages still lingers in this mingling of the divine and the mundane, in which every aspect of the visible world reflects, as in a mirror, images of the eternal.

Valerio Castello 1625-1672 • GENOESE

CHRIST WITH THE LITTLE CHILD, (detail), Bob Jones University, Greenville, South Carolina, pages 116-117.

Friend to poets, who celebrated his art in verse, Valerio Castello was one of the most popular painters of his day. A native of Genoa, he studied with Fiasella, and probably admired the works of the exuberant, dramatic Correggio. Castello treated each inch of canvas as if it must be charged with vitality, and his brushwork—by itself—is almost demoniac in intensity. The Renaissance ideal of harmony between man and nature had spawned a curiosity about every aspect of life. Yet by the latter part of the seventeenth century the ideals of harmony and grace were forgotten. Instead, artists strove to dramatize, to make eye-catching the simplest theme or subject.

Castello combined a concentration on surface effects with elements from the Flemish master Rubens: strong colors, and interlocking figures moving in and out of space. Unlike Rubens, however, he lacked acute awareness of the muscular human body and its expressive potential. Blending his own choice of elements from several painters, Castello is characteristic of many of the eclectic artists of this period.

Gerard David c. 1460-1523 • FLEMISH

Although one of the most successful and admired artists of his time, Gerard David was completely forgotten soon after his death. For over three hundred years he was known only as one of the anonymous 'masters' of the early Northern Renaissance. Not until the nineteenth century was he brought to light as an individual painter, by an English historian studying the city records in the archives of Bruges.

He had come to Bruges in 1484, probably from his native Holland. Although neither his birthplace nor date of birth are known precisely, it is believed he was born near Utrecht about 1460. This date is substantiated by the evidence of a self-portrait in a painting of 1509 in which he appears to be near fifty. He was, therefore, a young man in his late twenties when he arrived in Bruges and must have already achieved some distinction, for he was quickly admitted to the Painters Guild.

During the next ten years he rose rapidly within the guild, working on numerous commissions. He is said to have been the first master to keep a number of assistants and pupils working under his direction and reproducing his compositions, a practice Rubens was to exploit a hundred years later. In 1501, David became Dean, or President, of the Guild. His marriage to Cornelia Cnoop, a miniaturist and daughter of the Dean of the Goldsmiths Guild, no doubt added to his prestige and social standing.

David lived and worked in Bruges for forty years. He received commissions from the magistrates and prosperous burghers of that city and also from France, Italy, Spain and Portugal. In 1515, when Bruges began to decline in favor of Antwerp as the great commercial center of Western Europe, David established a workshop there, although he remained all his life a citizen of Bruges. By the time of his death in 1523 his reputation had been widely established as an artist of great talent and as a leader of his school, succeeding to the position of importance previously held by Memling, who had died a decade after David's arrival in Bruges. He was, in fact, the last great painter of the prolific Bruges school.

David was almost exclusively a painter of religious themes, especially the Virgin and Child and the early years of Jesus, which he painted with a gentle lyrical feeling and deep religious sentiment. One of his finest works, *The Baptism of Christ,* shows John baptising Jesus in the River Jordan, which has become a clear stream flowing through a peaceful Flemish landscape. In the background are two scenes: John preaching to the people of Christ's coming and Jesus appearing to his disciples in a small wood. The careful rendering of every detail, so characteristic of the Flemish style, reflects not only the painter's close observation of nature, but also the religious feeling of the time. The world of nature, seen as God's creation, is celebrated and glorified by the painter through a faithful and loving representation of it down to the smallest blade of grass and ripple on the surface of the water.

C. W. E. Dietrich 1712-1774 • GERMAN

Christian Wilhelm Ernst Dietrich was born at Weimar in 1712, the son of a court painter and miniaturist, Johann George Dietrich. After studying with his father, he went to Dresden to study under Alexander Thiele, a well-known landscape painter of that time. He soon gravitated to the court of Augustus II, King of Saxony, who sent him to Italy and the Netherlands to study, where he learned to imitate the old masters, a skill which he acquired with great alacrity. He became especially adept in the manner of Rembrandt, even to the reproduction of that master's signature and fictitious dates on a number of his own works.

In 1741, Dietrich was appointed court painter to Augustus III, receiving a yearly stipend which required him to produce four pictures a year. In addition to his paintings, he produced a number of engravings, also in the styles of various earlier artists, his favorites being Ostade and again Rembrandt. Dietrich was much admired in his time and considered a superb technician as well as an especially fine colorist.

He became custodian of the Dresden Gallery in 1746, where fifty-two of his canvases and panels still hang in a room reserved for them. He also served as Professor at the Academy of Art and directed the painting school at the famous Meissen Porcelain factory.

Gerbrand van den Eeckhout 1621-1674 · DUTCH

Born in Amsterdam, the son of a prosperous goldsmith, Gerbrand van den Eeckhout studied with Rembrandt at the age of fourteen. For the next five years, he developed his drawing skills in a vast number of sensitive etchings. He also learned to copy the close-knit, small-scale figures of Rembrandt's Biblical paintings in oils of his own. Van den Eeckhout's tones are less golden than his master's, and his characters are less sharply defined and dramatically posed. Yet there is delicacy, compassion and an exceptional sense of composition in van den Eeckhout's paintings that have made them appreciated as more than slavish copies.

In the mid-seventeenth century there was little or no market for oil paintings on religious themes, and van den Eeckhout's career as an artist was unique for his time. His father's wealth and position made him financially independent, enabling him to undertake historical and Biblical subjects in the manner of his master. Yet he also responded to the demand of Amsterdam's new middle class for portraits. He acquired a reputation as a portrait painter, and in these works departed from his reproduction of Rembrandt's unconventional style, tending more to the simple and popular manner of de Hooch and Terborch.

Van den Eeckhout outlived Rembrandt by five years, being one of the few old friends who remained close to the master during the final isolated period of Rembrandt's life.

Cornelis Engelbrechtsz 1468-1533 · DUTCH

The son of a wood-engraver, Cornelis Engelbrechtsz (also spelled Engelbertsz; Engelbrechtsen) was born at Leyden, and worked there all his life. He maintained a busy shop in which Aertgen van Leyden and the more famous Lucas van Leyden were probably trained.

Very few of Engelbrechtsz's works are in existence today. It is known, however, that he painted mostly subjects from the New Testament. Carel van Mander, the historian on early Dutch art, mentions as Engelbrechtsz's masterpiece a triptych, now lost, the center of which represented the Lamb of the Apocalypse. He also comments that Engelbrechtsz may be the first artist of his country to have painted exclusively in oil.

Additionally, it is known that Engelbrechtsz designed stained glass, and was a member of 'la garde bourgeoise' at Leyden, the class of burghers immortalized by Rembrandt in his painting, *The Night Watch.*

The artist lived during a period of transition in the art of the Low Countries. His work reflects this transition in its blending of elements from both the contained, precise early Netherlandish style (with extensive use of interiors) and later more developed movement and complex use of space explored by Brueghel and Rubens.

Domenico Fiasella 1589-1669 · GENOESE

Born at Sarzana in the Genoese state (he is sometimes known as 'il Sarzeno') Domenico Fiasella received his first training from his father, a goldsmith, and then studied briefly with two minor Genoese painters. He went to Rome, where he remained over ten years studying classical statues and the works of Raphael, Andrea del Sarto and Caravaggio. Fiasella's use of dramatic shafts of light and his vivid groupings recall especially Caravaggio.

Returning to Genoa, Fiasella acquired great favor with the public, both as a portrait-painter and a depictor of Biblical and mythological themes. He painted the canopy of the church of the Annunciation and other works for the churches of Genoa. By 1627, he was considered the major artist of the city.

In the years that followed, Fiasella received commissions from Naples, from Messina and from as far away as Spain. The Princess Maria who had never consented to let herself be painted, came to Mantua to sit for him; while there, the Duke of Mantua tried to persuade Fiasella to take permanent residence in his city.

The artist lived a long and active life. At the age of seventy-four, he undertook the painting of a vast canvas depicting the ravages caused in Genoa by the plague. He died at eighty, an honored and respected citizen of his native state.

Jean Fouquet c. 1420-c. 1480 • FRENCH

A prolific miniature painter in the great Franco-Flemish tradition and a remarkably candid portraitist, Jean Fouquet was born in Tours sometime between 1415 and 1425. The circumstances of his birth were to be a source of difficulty to him in his early years; he was the illegitimate son of a priest and an unmarried woman, a condition which made it impossible for him to receive any money from the Church without a special dispensation from the Pope. To this end he left France for Rome about 1445, after having completed his apprenticeship with Haincelin de Haguenau, the outstanding miniaturist of the School of Paris. His application to the church must have been granted, for in Rome he was commissioned, in spite of his youth, to paint a portrait of Pope Eugene IV. This work astonished the Italians by its great vividness, "seeming to be almost alive," as a contemporary account relates.

Fouquet stayed in Italy until 1448, absorbing certain elements of the developing Renaissance style but without imitating any particular painter or school. His adaptation of Italian forms was extremely selective. By fusing a general Italian breadth of feeling with the Franco-Flemish miniature technique which he had learned in Paris, he created a new and distinctive personal style.

On his return to France in 1448, Fouquet settled once more in Tours, the favorite residence of the King and his court. The talented young artist who had painted the Pope's portrait was immediately welcomed by King Charles VII, beginning a royal patronage which was to last all of Fouquet's life. He and numerous assistants were kept busy painting miniatures and manuscript illuminations, as well as the many portraits required by the vanity of the court. He painted the King, haughty and contemptuous, and other equally unsmiling members of the royal entourage. In his most famous painting, *The Virgin and Child,* Mary is represented in the likeness of the King's mistress, the beautiful Agnes Sorel.

Fouquet's prestige rose still higher in 1461 when Louis XI came to the throne. The production of his workshop was extended to include the design of all new public buildings, the organization and decoration of receptions for important visitors, the staging of mystery plays, and the drawing of designs for sculptures and stained glass windows. In effect, Fouquet became the artistic director of all Tours. Finally, in 1475, after almost twenty-five years in the service of the French court, he was officially named Painter of the King.

Fouquet was a realist. He was a painter of religious and historical scenes, yet he was neither a deeply pious man nor a troubled mystic. His temperament was not visionary but observing. He had a special talent for grasping the essential quality of people and objects and for setting them down with quick, sure strokes. The lively figures which so densely populate his delicate landscapes, whether angels or devils, peasants or knights, are all everyday people of the earthly race of the Île de France.

VESPASIAN MARCHES AGAINST THE JEWS, *miniature, (detail), Bibliothèque Nationale, Paris,* page **22.**

Lucas van Gassel c. 1500-1555 • FLEMISH

Lucas van Gassel is one of a group of painters who laid the foundation for the development of landscape painting as a separate genre. He was born at Helmont, but resided chiefly at Brussels, and probably died there. Gassel is thought to have finished his apprenticeship about 1520, although his earliest known picture was done in 1538. Primarily, he is remarkable for the predominance of the natural world in his religious paintings, and for his paintings which are wholly landscape. Some of these were executed in oil, others in water color. The oil paintings suggest an influence of the water color technique in their lightness and transparency. All portray a world of fairy-tale peacefulness; pure and gentle in feeling, with an almost flat perspective, they resemble the work of the landscape artist, Joachim Patinir.

Christ Appearing to His Disciples on the Sea of Tiberius is attributed to van Gassel with some uncertainty. In conception and design, it recalls a work by Konrad Witz, although its blue-green tonality and dwarf-like figures are distinctive of van Gassel. Patinir, van Gassel and Witz all painted not only the land but also the sea for the first time in any breadth or detail since the Greeks. Rising up like a vertical wall, yet spread out so as to create the impression of a bird's eye view, the painted bodies of water in these artists' works maintain a geometrically straight line on their horizons.

CHRIST APPEARING TO HIS DISCIPLES ON THE SEA OF TIBERIUS, *(detail), Wadsworth Atheneum, Hartford, Conn.,* pages **94-95.**

It is interesting to observe the special way in which Northern painters of this period solved the problem of depicting the Holy Land, a country which none of the Renaissance painters actually visited. Earlier artists, such as David, filled the background of their religious painting with landscape they saw around them, rendered with painstaking fidelity. Beginning with such painters as Jan Swart and van Gassel, the backgrounds assumed greater relative importance within the canvas, and were treated with more expressiveness and a greater play of imagination. The painter no longer had to be 'natural.' Rather, he aimed to gratify the curiosity of Flemish flat-landers about foreign lands and regions. Thus, other-worldly themes found their counterpart in settings of an equally transcendental nature.

Giorgione 1477-1510 • VENETIAN

THE MADONNA READING, *Ashmolean Museum, Oxford, England, page 56.*

Bernard Berenson, the distinguished scholar and historian, wrote of Giorgione: "his pictures are the perfect reflex of the Renaissance at its height, [when] its over-boisterous passions had quieted down into a sincere appreciation of beauty and of human relations."

Giorgione was born Zorzo Barbarelli 'del Castelfranco,' that is, of Castelfranco—a village in Trevisan near the Italian Alps. As a boy, the pastoral meadows and running waters of this region must have impressed him deeply. While still young, and poor, Giorgio (or Giorgione, 'The Great George,' as he later came to be called) went to Venice. There he received employment in the workshop of Bellini where he met Titian, among others. At the age of eighteen he was able to copy his master's style with sufficient skill to provide the companion pieces to Bellini's *Allegory* at the Villa Medici. By the time he was twenty, he was almost certainly painting on his own.

His early work consists of religious paintings, as well as a number of portraits. It was as a portrait painter that his fame grew: the most illustrious names of Venice came to pose for him, and he had all the commissions he could accept.

As the years passed, he completed a number of canvases that were neither religious subjects nor portraits. They might combine, for example, a nude with landscape, in which one is not more important than the other—but in which both contribute to a mood of rare harmony between woman and nature. In some, the clouds are alive with thunder; in others, the horizon is peaceful. These pictures are sensual and softly coloured, with a stillness about them; yet the stillness is almost audible, as if a passage in music were suddenly suspended. Interestingly, Giorgione's love of the arts extended to music: he was known to sing and to play the lute.

Revolutionary in concept and execution, these unclassifiable works are no less impressive than his allegorical paintings, many of them frescoes commissioned for the palaces of the Venetian nobility. They have a similar quality, being composed of living, almost breathing people, as alive as the natural settings which they inhabit. Yet both subject and setting, as in the paintings of nudes, are intensely hushed.

In the year 1510 the plague swept through Venice, taking Giorgione as one of its victims. He was then at the height of his prominence, and only thirty-three years of age.

The style of this High Renaissance artist has been described as a blending of a refined poetic feeling that Giorgione found in Bellini, with a sense of color and elegance he took from Carpaccio. Actually, there is no precedent for the particular quality of Giorgione's work. He saw in man the same sweetness and inner movement he felt existed in nature. His unique sense of grace and form finds its origins, if anywhere, in Classical culture and art.

His *Madonna Reading* is an especially intriguing work. It is the depiction of a traditional figure in an unconventional pose, with the Madonna concentrating on a book rather than the Holy Child. In a period of such intense intellectual activity as the Renaissance, it is not inappropriate that the Madonna is reading. Yet Giorgione may have been indulging in that curious combination of enigma and surprise which is typical of him. Part of the charm of his works is the startling effect of seeing a combination of disparate elements, such as a landscape with a nude, or a Madonna with a book.

Giorgione's influence on the Venetian painters equalled that of Michelangelo and Raphael on the Romans. Unhappily, few of his works have escaped deterioration and destruction.

Hugo van der Goes c. 1440-1482 • FLEMISH

Hugo van der Goes experienced in his short, tragic life the passionate spiritual involvement which permeates and transfigures his work. He combined the expressiveness of Rogier van der Weyden with the infinitesimal realism of van Eyck. This synthesis created a new, powerful form to articulate his deeply personal religious feeling.

Hugo was a citizen of Ghent, an ancient city with a long artistic history. In its cathedral stood the great *Ghent Altarpiece,* painted by Jan van Eyck eight years before Hugo's birth. This painting had a far-reaching influence on all early Flemish painting, and a particularly strong effect on the young Hugo while he was studying there. He attained his mastership in 1467 and one year later was called to Bruges to assist in decorating that city for the marriage of Charles the Bold and Margaret of York. His subsequent rise to fame was spectacular. The following year he was put in charge of the decoration of Ghent for Charles' state visit, a function he was to repeat in four succeeding years. Then, in 1474, still a relatively junior member of the Guild, he was elected its Dean.

His greatest work, *The Adoration of the Shepherds,* was commissioned by the agent and banker of the Medici in Bruges, Tommaso Portinari, who sent it to Florence. There the painting had a tremendous effect on the Italian painters who flocked to see it. They were astonished by the microscopic realism of every detail and dramatic characterization of real-life people, so much more earthy and human than their own idealized types.

Hugo's career was then at its peak; his name was spoken with awe and wonder not only in Flanders but in far away Italy as well. Yet he suddenly turned his back on fame and withdrew from the world; in 1476 he entered a monastery near Brussels. Many explanations have been given for his sudden withdrawal: his moodiness and introversion, his overzealousness alternating with periods of depression; his exaggerated sensitivity. All of them indicate an intensely emotional nature and forbode the tragedy which was to overtake him in the last years of his life. He continued to paint in the monastery but became prey to fits of melancholy, obsessed by impatience to transmit to canvas works which existed only in his mind. More and more frequently he soothed his anguish with wine. As the years passed, his depression grew; he felt himself eternally damned, and attempted suicide. The prior, "suspecting that Hugo was struck with the affliction that had tormented King Saul and recalling how he was appeased by David's playing on the harp..." had music played in Hugo's presence in an attempt to cure him. Despite all efforts, his madness increased (traces of it are evident in his last works) and he died in the monastery in 1482.

Although Hugo continued the Flemish naturalistic tradition, his is far from a simple realism. Acute in its psychological penetration, his work emanates a natural vitality and spiritual fervor which illumine the mask of appearances.

Benozzo Gozzoli 1420-1497 • FLORENTINE

Although a contemporary of the early Renaissance painters, Benozzo Gozzoli remained in spirit a Medieval artist all his life, carrying on the Gothic tradition of courtly and decorative story telling to the end of the fifteenth century.

He was born in Florence and is known to have been studying painting in 1442, probably by then in the last years of his apprenticeship. He must also have been trained as a sculptor, for in 1444 he signed a three-year contract to work under the famous Lorenzo Ghiberti on the second pair of bronze doors for the Baptistory in Florence, the work which Michelangelo was later to call "The Gates of Paradise." In 1447 he went to Rome as an assistant to Fra Angelico, and completed a set of frescoes in Orvieto, which Angelico had apparently abandoned. For the next decade he traveled throughout central Italy, painting frescoes on the walls of various churches and public buildings in Rome, Viterbo and Perugia. In 1459 he returned to Florence, then at the height of its importance as a center of art and learning under the powerful patronage of the Medici family.

The work for which Gozzoli is most famous is a fresco panorama, *The Journey of the Magi,* painted for the Medici in the chapel of the Riccardi palace in Florence. This chapel originally contained an altarpiece by Fra Filippo Lippi depicting the Adoration of the Christ

PORTINARI ALTARPIECE: THE ADORATION OF THE SHEPHERDS, *(detail of Joseph and Mary on the Road to Bethlehem)* pages 22-23; *(detail of Angels)* page 30; *(detail of St. Thomas)* pages 128-129. *Uffizi Gallery, Florence.*

PORTRAIT OF A MAN, *(detail),* *Metropolitan Museum of Art, New York,* page 134.

JOURNEY OF THE MAGI, *(detail), Riccardi Palace, Florence,* page 43.

Child, and Gozzoli's frescoes were conceived as an accompaniment to the altarpiece. The Magi and their attendants, followed by a long caravan of donkeys and camels, are shown on their journey to Bethlehem. A mixture of naturalism and fairy tale, this religious painting is also a portrait gallery of the great men of the time. The Three Kings are represented as Lorenzo de Medici, the Emperor of Byzantium, and the Patriarch of Constantinople. Behind them rides Lorenzo's father Piero, followed by the grandfather Cosimo, the domineering founder of the Medici dynasty. Gozzoli has painted his own face near the end of the procession as if to say, "I was there, too."

After finishing this work, Gozzoli went to nearby San Gimignano and painted frescoes of the life of St. Augustine, as well as a panel painting of St. Sebastian commissioned by the townspeople as a protection against the plague of 1464. The last part of his life was devoted to a vast cycle of twenty-five scenes from the Old Testament in the Campo Santo at Pisa.

Marten van Heemskerck 1498-1574 • DUTCH

THE ENTOMBMENT OF CHRIST, (detail of a mourning woman), Royal Museums of Fine Arts, Brussels, pages 48-49.

Born Marten van Veen in the village of Heemskerck, near Haarlem, this painter has come to be known as Marten van Heemskerck.

Marten was apprenticed by his father, a farmer, to Cornelis Willensz, a Haarlem painter. While still young, he left Willensz, hoping to absorb something of the Italian Renaissance style from one of the Dutch or Flemish artists who had gone to Italy. Coming to the workshop of Jan van Scorel, he proved an exceptionally able pupil. Tradition has it his progress and skill in imitating his master so excited the jealousy of van Scorel that Marten was chased out of the workshop. Yet he stayed long enough to acquire his master's understanding of the Italian style, derived from Raphael, whom van Scorel had succeeded as keeper of the treasures of the Vatican.

In 1535, Marten arrived in Rome, then struggling to reestablish itself after the disastrous sack of the city by French and Spanish troops in 1527. Marten became absorbed in a study of Raphael's last works, as well as Michelangelo's monumental sculpture and great frescoes of the Sistine Chapel. *The Last Judgment* had just been completed, and its powerfully drawn figures and exaggerated movements deeply moved Marten.

In Rome, he was also exposed to the new Mannerist style, a development and distortion of the emotional elements of Raphael and Michelangelo, in which every detail of figure and clothing express the tension and pain of inner feelings. When Marten returned to Haarlem, he began to paint on a larger scale, with figures more heroic and impassioned. Line and color became both a means of describing form with great accuracy and the direct expression of intense emotions.

Marten married shortly after his return from Rome. In later years he designed stained glass windows and completed altarpieces for churches in Alkmaar, Haarlem and Ghent. His popularity grew as a portraitist, and he became President of the Guild of Painters. Marten fled to Amsterdam in 1572 when the Spanish seized Haarlem, returning there only in the year of his death.

By his use of line and color as direct expressive means, Marten is allied with the great German painters of the preceding generation, Dürer and Grunewald, who also explored the potential of the human figure in deeply religious and powerful paintings.

Gerard von Honthorst 1590-1656 • DUTCH

ADORATION OF THE CHILD, (detail), Uffizi Gallery, Florence, pages 24-25.

THE HOLY FAMILY IN THE CARPENTER SHOP, Bob Jones University, Greenville, South Carolina, pages 58-59.

Gerard von Honthorst kept to the tradition of Dutch artists who used Italian painting as their inspiration. Born in Utrecht, then the center of newly-established Protestantism, von Honthorst admired the new life which contemporary Italians, following Caravaggio, were then putting into religious themes.

His first teacher was Abraham Bloemaert, a Dutchman with a "strongly Italianate flavor." At the age of twenty the artist himself went to Rome to learn the Italian style first-hand. In Rome he executed, among other works, frescoes for Santa Maria della Scala. Von Honthorst copied Caravaggio's large, spontaneously drawn figures in dark tones with strongly contrasting, almost eerie, light and shadows. The Italian's religious paintings were not idealized representations of the characters of the New Testament, nor were von Honthorst's. They showed real people, modeled on lower-class figures whose flesh, muscles and physical irregularities were caught by the artist's brush, as if by a camera. Yet von Honthorst's works emphasize an intimacy and sweetness of tone that recall earlier Catholic painting of both Flemish and Italian origin.

Von Honthorst was elected Dean of the Guild of Saint Luke after his return to Utrecht. He also opened a school, which was widely attended. He painted genre scenes and historical works, as well as incidents from the New Testament—all with the same direct naturalism he had learned in Italy. Utrecht was then under the protection of the English Earl, and von Honthorst's reputation spread to England. In 1628 he was invited by Charles I to adorn the interior of the Palace of Whitehall with allegorical paintings. He then returned to Holland to decorate the palace of the Hague, and completed a series of pictures illustrating Danish history for the King of Denmark.

In later years the artist devoted himself entirely to portraits, and they were much sought after. In 1637 he settled at the Hague as Painter to the Court. He died in his native city.

In Italy, von Honthorst came to be known as 'Gherardo della notte' (Gerald of the Night) for almost all his pictures were set at night, or by candlelight. Those that were not, set off subjects with dark backgrounds. Today, we admire that mastery of shadows which so dramatically reveals the humanity of man, portrayed with immediacy and directness.

J. A. D. Ingres 1780-1867 • FRENCH

In the latter part of the eighteenth century, French painting rose to the height of Neo-Classicism under the influence of the Napoleonic artist, Jacques Louis David. David's large, well-spaced canvases, with figures drawn in graceful, formal positions, attracted the admiration of many young artists. Among them was the brilliant student destined to take David's place as the leader of the forces of Classicism in the early part of the next century: Jean Auguste Dominque Ingres.

Born in the city of Montauban, Ingres was the son of an artist who wanted his child to become a musician. Ingres learned the violin at an early age and soon was able to support himself by playing in the Lyons orchestra. But Ingres was devoted to 'his father's business.' There is a story that he saw a copy of a Raphael Madonna, and thereafter vowed to become a painter. Whether or not the story is true, Ingres went to Paris in 1796 and entered the studio of David. After four years of study he received the Prix de Rome of 1801. Lack of finances, however, prevented him from taking advantage of the year's study in Rome until 1805. Once in Rome, Ingres found the fall of the Napoleonic dynasties in Rome had removed most of his potential patrons. Nevertheless, he earned pocket money by making line drawings of French visitors to Rome, and satisfied himself with visits to museums to see the works of Raphael and archaic sculpture. He also became fascinated by the flat linearism of Greek vases, a technique he began to apply to sketches and paintings of the nude—the perfect vehicle for his exploitation of line and form. His oils from this period reveal his work was already strongly linear and rhythmic, the overall effect enhanced by enamel-like surfaces.

In the early 1820's, Ingres received a commission for an altarpiece for the Cathedral of Montauban from the Administration of Fine Arts in France. When he came to Paris to see the completed work exhibited at the Salon of 1824, he found himself a great success. Ingres decided to stay and opened his own atelier.

In his school he laid down rules of art which a generation of students would follow devoutly: "form is the foundation and condition of everything; Raphael and the Greeks lead to the essence of beauty in nature; the ugly is the unnatural." In 1825, the year of David's death, Ingres was elected to the Institute. Vain and sensitive, he left Paris in 1834 when one of his most ambitious new works was badly received at the Salon, and accepted the offer of the Directorship of the French School at Rome.

Ingres returned to Paris in 1841 and was enthusiastically received. Twenty-five years of success followed, in which he completed a score of allegorical paintings, nudes and portraits

CHRIST AMONG THE ELDERS IN THE TEMPLE, *(detail), Musée Ingres, Montauban, France, pages* **68-69.**

in oil. His nudes, combining perfection of line and form with an extraordinary gift for reproducing the pale skin of his models, made his name famous. Placed in lush interiors in juxtaposition with strong, often dissonant colors and textures, these paintings exude a flavor of the Near East and the Orient.

In 1855 Ingres was promoted to the rank of Commander of the Legion of Honor and a room was reserved for his works at the International Exhibition. In his final years he continued to accept many commissions, including one from Queen Marie Aurelie for the Chapel at Bizy. This work, *Christ Among the Elders in the Temple* was completed at the age of eighty-two. Unusual for Ingres in its religious theme, its clearly-drawn figures and elaborately balanced composition are characteristic of his work.

After his death, a museum was opened in the artist's name in Montauban.

Delacroix, the leader of the opposing Romantics, said Ingres was "a Chinese or Japanese artist who had strayed into Greece." This comment may be read as approbation or condemnation, yet inherent in Delacroix's words is the realization that Ingres extended the boundaries of French painting. Ingres copied Giotto, Masaccio, and Byzantine mosaics when the Baroque and the High Renaissance were the only permissible styles to imitate. "The crude beginnings of certain arts are sometimes more perfect than perfected arts," he wrote. Ingres clearly believed this to be true, though he devoted his life to a re-appreciation of that most perfected of artists, Raphael.

Ingres' appropriate place in the history of art has been suggested by the following proportion: "Ingres is to Raphael as Haydn is to Mozart." If this judgment is questioned, it should be noted the equation was written by Ingres himself.

Jakob Jordaens 1593-1678 • FLEMISH

THE ADORATION OF THE SHEPHERDS, *(detail of a shepherd)*, *Kunsthalle, Hamburg, page* 31.

Born fifteen years after Rubens, Jakob Jordaens lived much of his lifetime in the shadow of the great Flemish master. Assisted and influenced by Rubens, he nevertheless developed a reputation and style completely his own, and when Rubens died in 1640, he inherited most of the important commissions of the day.

Jordaens' father, a draper, could not give his son the extensive education other artists such as Rubens and Van Dyck had received. Neither could Jordaens go to Italy as a young man, as other Flemish artists had done. Instead, at the age of fourteen he entered the studio of Adam van Noort, Rubens' teacher, and continued studying and copying the works of the Italian masters in Flanders. After eight years of apprenticeship, he married van Noort's daughter, Catherine. Jordaens, van Noort and Catherine now began to live together under one roof, an arrangement which continued for some time. In 1621 Jordaens became a member of the Guild of St. Luke, and a few years later became the Guild's leader.

Jordaens was a prolific and versatile painter. He provided designs for the Flemish tapestry makers, and in 1535, at the request of Rubens, decorated some triumphal arches. In addition to religious subjects, he also painted illustrations of proverbs and genre pieces—scenes from the everyday life around him. In 1641 Jordaens received an important commission. The King of Spain had applied to Rubens for a series of cartoons to be executed in tapestry, but Rubens died before they could be completed. Jordaens was engaged to finish them, and thereafter his reputation on the continent seems to have been assured. Numbered among his patrons were both Charles I of England and the King of Sweden. He died at the age of eighty-five, a victim of the plague which ravaged Antwerp in 1678.

Inevitably, Jordaens' style shows the influence of Rubens, although his work as a whole is less heroic. Jordaens painted a lower class of Flemish life than depicted by Rubens and Van Dyck, but this was only natural. His life is known to have been filled with much merrymaking, feasts and drinking parties, and Jordaens used as models the people he saw and knew.

Jordaens was not without deep religious sentiments. He embraced Calvinism midway through life, though not so strongly that he refused commissions from Catholic churches. One of his favorite themes was *The Adoration of the Shepherds,* of which there are several versions. Here, his ability to capture the Flemish character is splendidly manifest in painting of an unusual depth and almost photographic immediacy.

Pieter van Lint 1609-1690 · FLEMISH

Pieter van Lint was born in Antwerp shortly after its ascendancy as the major port of Northern Europe. Trained under Roland Jacobsz, young van Lint was a Master of the great Guild of Antwerp by the age of twenty-four. Shortly afterwards he made his way to Rome where he acquired the friendship of a Cardinal, Domenico Ginnasio. Van Lint decorated the Cardinal's church in Ostia, the seaport of Rome, and stayed in Rome nine years, filling many other religious commissions. By the time he returned to his native soil, his name had traveled across the continent. He settled in Antwerp, opened a studio, married and became the father of two children. Prosperous and sought after, van Lint eventually came to include among his patrons such luminaries as King Christian IV of Denmark. When his wife died, he married his servant, and in the last ten years of his life, she gave him three children. He died at the age of eighty-one.

Van Lint's cool and restrained painting reflects the years the artist spent in Italy. In *Christ at the Pool of Bethesda,* his formal composition treats architecture as a backdrop in front of which his equally balanced actors pose. An instructive comparison may be made with Murillo's depiction of the same subject, painted during the same period. Again, a cloaked Christ gestures formally to the "man with an infirmity" (John, V:5). However, in Murillo's work the figures are painted with deep emotion and involvement. The Spanish artist brings the principals close to the spectator with the help of flowing line, strong illumination of the faces, and by their forward placement. Van Lint, on the other hand, makes of his canvas a presentation: interest in the main figures is subordinated to the composition of the whole, while the even distribution of light and flat modeling of the faces help to give the impression that the material worn by the subjects is more interesting to the painter than the subjects themselves.

CHRIST AT THE POOL OF BETHESDA, *(detail), Royal Museums of Fine Arts, Brussels, pages* 106-107.

Claude Lorrain 1600-1682 · FRENCH

The sense of mystery evoked by the delicate, detailed canvases of Claude Lorrain is reflected in existing accounts of his life.

Born Claude Gellée in a village on the Moselle in Vosges country (then called Lorraine) the artist came to be known as 'Claude Lorrain' or simply 'Claude'. His early years, disputed by conflicting biographers, may have been spent as apprentice to a local pastry-chef or an apprentice to his older brother Jean, an artist, at Fribourg on the Rhine. Claude was left an orphan at the age of twelve, and he found his way to Rome by the time he was fourteen. In Rome, he lived in the house of a Perugian landscape painter, Agostino Tassi. He looked after kitchen and household affairs, ground colors, cleaned palettes and brushes, and perhaps learned the art of perspective from Tassi.

Claude left Rome in the spring of 1625 and began a series of wanderings: to Venice, to Bavaria, back to Lorraine, then to Nancy and Marseilles. In these travels, Claude began to sketch in the open air. He made studies of landscape details, trees and rocks, each sketch detailing separate gradations of light. Claude is recognized as the first painter who dared look the sun in the face and who tried to paint it as he saw it.

The artist led an isolated existence when he settled in Rome again. At first, he met with little success; but in ten years' time, his work attracted one of the leading cardinals of the Papal court. This contact led to the reigning Pope Urban VII ordering four paintings from him. Ostensibly religious or historic scenes, these works betray Claude's passion for landscape. He would go into the country outside Rome in the afternoon, mix his colors while the effects of light were still before him, then go home to apply them to his work. Lorrain's landscapes bring this feeling of the open air onto canvas: even the sun and rain seem to be painted into his grass.

Claude's patrons eventually came to include the King of Spain, Pope Alexander VII, Pope Clement IX and many cardinals and princes. Yet Claude was reputedly often unhappy, beset by many misfortunes. He barely survived several long illnesses and a fall from a scaffolding. Worse, copyists and plagiarists called their work "original Claudes" and the artist

THE SERMON ON THE MOUNT, *Frick Collection, New York, pages* 124-125.

was forced to keep numbered sketches of his paintings to verify which were his own.

Claude and his workshop completed upwards of four hundred paintings. Most of them conform to an underlying scheme of composition in which the canvas is divided into a series of planes receding into space, culminating in what has been called a "luminous distance."

Claude saw a new relationship between man and nature. In his view, man no longer stood in the position of dominance, but was merely an element of the natural world, equal in importance to a rock or a tree. It is Claude who said, "I give my figures away, but I sell my landscapes." The artist gave so little thought to the people in his pictures that an assistant often painted them in.

In the eighteenth century, gentlemen carried a device called a 'Claude glass,' that they might see a landscape with "the golden tone of a Claude." In the nineteenth century, Impressionists hailed him as the first artist to note that a setting changes under varying aspects of light. Today, he is revered for the subtle quality of his brush that could capture equally the infinitesimal leaves of a spreading tree or the rolling clouds of a distant horizon, yet make the whole seem finally half-real and half-imagined.

Simon Marmion c. 1425-1489 • FRANCO-FLEMISH

A CHOIR OF ANGELS, *fragment from the St. Bertin Altarpiece, (detail), National Gallery, London. vaae 32.*

Simon Marmion was a manuscript illuminator and panel painter active in the last half of the fifteenth century in Northern France and the states of Burgundy. Born and apparently educated in Amiens, he is last heard of there in 1454 when he was head of a large and prosperous miniaturists' atelier. He worked later in Valenciennes, in Tournai, and at the court of the Dukes of Burgundy. He was among the many artists employed by Charles the Bold, Duke of Burgundy from 1467 to 1477, a generous patron of the arts. Charles' patronage attracted most of the great artists of his time: his portrait was painted by Rogier van der Weyden, and both Hugo van der Goes and Hans Memling worked on designs for the festivities in honor of his marriage to Princess Margaret of York. Marmion contributed to the celebration of this famous alliance, too. His panel painting of the *Pietà* bearing the arms of England and Burgundy, inscribed on the back with the initials of Charles and Margaret, was probably presented to them as a wedding gift in 1468.

Marmion's most important surviving work is the St. Bertin Altarpiece, formerly thought to be by Memling. It is now identified as Marmion's by its similarities to his manuscript illuminations. An elaborately gilded and jeweled series of panels painted between 1480 and 1490 for the Abbey of St. Bertin in St. Omer, France, the altarpiece disappeared from the church during the French Revolution. The panels were scattered and have never been reunited. The left and right wings were discovered in a baker's shop in St. Omer and were sent to Berlin; two small fragments representing angels later found their way to London.

Masaccio 1401-c. 1429 • FLORENTINE

THE TRIBUTE MONEY, *(detail), Brancacci Chapel, Santa Maria del Carmine, Florence, pages 102-103.*

Vasari, the great biographer of the Renaissance, says of Masaccio in his *Lives of the Artists:* "the works produced before his time should be called paintings; but his performance, when compared with those works might be designated life, truth and nature." In his short life Masaccio transformed the painting of his time, carrying it to an unheard of naturalism and drama. Before Masaccio only Giotto had presented tangible human figures in a natural world; after him came the whole development of the Renaissance.

Masaccio was born in 1401 in a small town near Florence. He was, again according to Vasari, "remarkably absent and careless of externals as one who, having fixed his whole mind and thought on art, cared little for himself, the cares of the world and the general interests of life." Perhaps this negligence of himself gave rise to the nickname 'Masaccio,' a slightly derogatory form of his real name, Tommaso. He was a pupil of Masolino with whom he collaborated on the famous frescoes of Santa Maria del Carmine; but he soon surpassed his master, just as Leonardo was to transcend Verrocchio some fifty years later.

Much of Masaccio's work has been destroyed. Many of the frescoes have deteriorated badly, but those which have survived reveal the power and dignity of his vision, stripped of all but the essential. His greatest work, the frescoes in the Brancacci chapel representing the Expulsion from Eden and scenes from the life of St. Peter, created a great commotion in Florence when they were completed. At first unintelligible to many, they became the model for contemporary painters and those of following generations—Leonardo, Raphael and Michelangelo—who came to study them. In *The Tribute Money,* the simplified forms and economy of gesture give the figures of Christ and his Apostles a great solemnity and dramatic intensity. Divine, yet human, they seem depictions of real people in a real space, solid three-dimensional forms which for the first time in the history of painting cast shadows on the ground.

Masaccio left Florence for Rome soon after completing these frescoes, but little is known of the work he did there. He arrived in 1427, but by November 1429 he was dead. The circumstances of his sudden death were mysterious, and it was rumored that he had been poisoned—a not uncommon occurrence then. In less than ten years he had created a new form for painting, an achievement so abrupt and so towering that it was hardly understood by his contemporaries.

Masaccio stands today as one of the revolutionary figures who created the Renaissance style in Florence. Yet like many artists of our time, he worked in comparative isolation. He lived in the corner of a shop, had almost no personal possessions, and died heavily in debt.

Jan Massys 1509-1575 • FLEMISH

Born in 1509, Jan Massys did not share the congenial artistic environment which his father Quentin had enjoyed all his life. Growing up under the elder Massys' tutelage, he soon mastered the craft of painting; and in 1531 he became a master of the Antwerp Guild.

Jan had been only eight years old when Martin Luther nailed his ninety-five theses to the door of the Church of Wittenberg, and the Reformation was soon in full tide over the Netherlands. The same year Jan was made a master painter, Charles V revived his 1529 edict against all Lutherans, Anabaptists and other Protestants. In 1534 the order went out to expel all Anabaptists from Antwerp, all the men remaining after a given date to be burned alive and the women to be drowned in the river Scheldt. Jan, then twenty-five, was already infected with the new ideas, yet not until 1543 did he go too far in voicing his beliefs. In that year he was banished from Flanders for his heretical opinions.

He probably spent his exile in France and Italy but little is known of his life during his long fifteen years away from his native country. In 1550 he requested permission to return. This was the year of the Edict of Blood—by which any printer, seller, reader or owner of a work by Luther, Zwingli or Calvin (or anyone secretly entertaining their opinions), was to be burned and his property confiscated. The time was hardly propitious for Jan's return and his request was refused. Not until 1558 did he return to Antwerp, still apparently a secret Protestant.

In that same year he painted the panel *Joseph and Mary Turned from the Inn,* an unusual subject in Christian iconography. Perhaps his motive for selecting this theme can be found in the double meaning then being inserted into the painting of orthodox Christian themes by many painters who were secretly Protestant. The scene at the inn was one of these crypto-Protestant subjects and could be interpreted as an allegory of Rome's refusal to admit the Protestants into the Church. Thus it served as a hidden but incisive attack on the Ecclesiastical authorities, while masquerading as a simple illustration of the Biblical narrative.

Quentin Massys c. 1465-1530 • FLEMISH

Born toward the end of the great period of early Flemish painting, Massys belongs to the generation after Memling, Hugo van der Goes and Dirk Bouts. He was ten years old when Bouts died at Louvain, but his style was probably formed in the Bouts tradition.

Quentin Massys might never have become a painter but for two things—he fell sick, and he fell in love. Until he was twenty years old he followed the trade of blacksmith in his native Louvain. Then—as a contemporary story goes—a friend brought him popular woodcuts to

JOSEPH AND MARY TURNED FROM THE INN, *Royal Museum of Fine Arts, Antwerp, page* 23.

THE ADORATION OF THE MAGI, *Metropolitan Museum of Art, New York, page* 42.

color when he was sick in bed, and he began to paint. Later, he fell in love with the daughter of a local artist; but she first rejected him, reluctant to marry a humble smith. So Massys gave up his former work, determined to become a painter. They married, the following year.

For a young and ambitious painter, Louvain was too far away from the center of artistic activity. Antwerp was rapidly becoming the most important commercial center of the Netherlands and its rich merchants, eager to gain prestige, were fostering the arts. Massys moved to Antwerp and in 1493 he was admitted to the Guild of Painters. By the time he was thirty he had his own large workshop with a number of pupils, a remarkable achievement for a man who had started his career when most painters had already completed their apprenticeships.

In prosperous sixteenth century Antwerp the most successful painters became rich and lived in elegance. Massys soon found it necessary to expand his quarters in order to house both his prospering workshop and growing family, and he bought a house and garden on one street and two houses on another. The former was decorated both inside and out with frescoes, which were pointed out to Dürer as one of the sights of the town when he visited there in 1520.

Sought out by such artists as Dürer and Holbein, Massys was also a man of humanist culture, the friend of Erasmus and Sir Thomas More, whose portraits he painted. Made more susceptible to contemporary ideas by his contacts with such scholars, Massys was instrumental in transmitting many of the cultural and artistic achievements of the Italian High Renaissance to Northern Europe. His work shows the influence of the Venetian school in its strong and glowing color, but even more profound was the impact of Leonardo, from whom he learned to paint figures of increasing individualism. The deeply personal faces and triangular grouping of the Madonna and Child and the kneeling King in the *Adoration of the Magi* are strongly reminiscent of Leonardo's central figures in his unfinished painting of the same subject.

Massys had a great influence on subsequent Flemish painting. In his acutely drawn and haunting faces, there is already a heightened feeling for characterization which foreshadows Brueghel, Rubens and the psychological penetration of Rembrandt.

Master of the Magdalen Legend c. 1500 • FLEMISH

THE HOLY FAMILY, *(detail),* *Royal Museum of Fine Arts, Antwerp, page* **57.**

The Master of the Magdalen Legend is one of the many anonymous fifteenth and sixteenth century painters whose unsigned, undocumented works, have survived, but whose identities have not. These painters, admired mostly for their story-telling qualities, are usually named for a distinctive work or subject matter. In the case of the present artist, his name comes from a number of scenes from the Legend of Mary Magdalen, the stories which popular imagination has added to the Gospel account to embellish the life of the saint.

He is supposed to have been active in Brussels between the years 1480 and 1530. In addition to the paintings of the Magdalen, his works include portrayals of the Madonna, saints and angels, and scenes from the early years of Jesus, as well as a number of portraits of court personages.

Stylistically, the Master of the Magdalen Legend is a belated follower of Rogier van der Weyden, from whose works he adopted certain expressive gestures and facial types. The painting of *The Holy Family* represents a rarely depicted scene in the life of Jesus. The artist's imagination was given free play with material found in the popular thirteenth century *Meditations on the Life of Christ,* a poetic and sentimental elaboration of Jesus' life. Although the subject matter is uncommon, the treatment is typical of the Netherlands with its naïvely descriptive realism. In their simple faith, the early Flemish painters pictured the Biblical events as taking place in their own homes, with Joseph and Mary in the guise of contemporary townspeople, surrounded by everyday articles of household use. Gone are the haloes and stiff formality of the early Middle Ages, replaced by a new intimacy and naturalness reflecting a changed religious concept. Less majestic and aloof, the great figures of the Christian story have come down to earth, and the religious mystery transformed into a personal drama. The divine world is no longer an abstraction, but a living reality, in direct contact with daily life.

Hans Memling c. 1435-1494 • FLEMISH

At the time of his death, Memling was regarded as "the most accomplished and excellent painter in Christendom." His fame had spread far beyond Flanders, his adopted country. But a hundred years after his death he was completely forgotten. Even in Bruges, where he spent his whole life, nothing was known of him; and of all his works, only one was to be found in the city.

Both his name and family are of Dutch origin, but Memling (or Memlinc in Flemish) was born in a small village of northwestern Germany. It is not known where he was apprenticed; perhaps he studied at Cologne, for he later rendered the architecture of that city with a precision and fidelity which could only have been the result of direct observation. Similar painted details of the Brussels Town Hall substantiate the belief he studied there under Rogier van der Weyden, at least for a few years before that master's death in 1464. By 1467 Memling was in Bruges, where he became a citizen, and was accepted in the Painters Guild. Within three years he was appointed Town Painter. He married the daughter of a wealthy burgher, and in 1480 bought a large stone house with two small adjacent houses to contain his growing workshop. He was constantly working on commissions for the city, the Church, wealthy Flemish bankers, and for numerous foreign merchants who lived in Bruges. The city records reveal that he was one of the hundred and forty richest citizens— those paying the highest taxes in the town. Far from being a struggling painter at odds with the world around him, Memling was a highly honored citizen of his time. He was a good businessman as well as an artist, and worked within the regulations of a well-defined craft, painting themes fully understood by the people of his time.

The Seven Joys of the Virgin, completed in 1480, is painted in the spirit of the miniaturists and reflects the influence of the popular mystery plays (in which scenes were represented simultaneously on different parts of the stage). In a series of interconnected scenes, the painting, measuring six by three feet, shows the whole story of the Nativity from the Annunciation to the Flight into Egypt, as well as later events from the Gospels, culminating in the Death and Assumption of the Virgin. The figures weave in and out of the landscape and make-believe architecture in well-ordered patterns. Nature, tamed and serene, exists as a setting for the people who move with animated grace and gentle, restrained emotion. Neither man nor nature seems to dominate; they exist together in complete harmony and peace. The Christian story finds here a whole world for its stage, a naturalistic land and people of the imagination, where a religious truth and an historical event are recreated.

SEVEN JOYS OF THE VIRGIN, *(detail of the Wise Men at the Court of Herod)* pages **38-39**; *(detail of the Adoration of the Christ Child) pages* **40-41.** *Alte Pinakothek, Munich.*

Bartolomé Esteban Murillo 1617-1682 • SPANISH

Murillo is considered the master of the Spanish Baroque style in its more sentimental aspect.

Born into a humble family in Seville, he was left an orphan when his parents died from effects of the plague. Placed under the guardianship of his uncle at the age of eleven, Murillo spent hours in museums studying masters who were to have a great influence on his style: Rubens, van Dyck, Raphael and Correggio. His uncle, a struggling doctor, was dismayed at the boy's artistic leanings. But another relative, Juan del Castillo, taught Murillo drawing until the age of twenty-two. Then, departing for Cadiz, del Castillo left Murillo to his own resources. At the 'feria' or public-fair of Seville, Murillo received his first chance to develop a public. He sold paintings of madonnas and saints as well as non-religious works, depictions of country people and beggar boys. This division of his output into two groups was to last his lifetime.

Murillo moved to Madrid in 1642, and was soon taken under the wing of the great Velasquez, who introduced him to the King. After a year or two of study he returned to Seville, where he undertook the painting of eleven pictures for a Franciscan convent. These works, painted in the period of what is known as his 'frio' or cold style, are rather hard and linear, but they gained him a great following.

In 1648 he married a lady of noble birth, who later presented him with two sons and one daughter. She is also credited with having deepened his religious sentiments. For a time, he dressed himself in rags and worked at a home for travelers and the underprivileged.

CHRIST HEALING THE PARALYTIC AT THE POOL OF BETHESDA, *(details), National Gallery, London, pages* **104, 105.**

Murillo settled in Seville, where, against much opposition, he put forward the idea of a Public Academy of Art. During the 1660's, he developed what is known as his 'vaporoso' style, in which the outlines and careful drawing of his earlier work were replaced by a blending of light and shade, with great atmospheric effect.

By now Murillo had become so attached to the city of his birth he refused to leave. But in 1682, at the age of sixty-four, he was persuaded to travel to Cadiz to paint an altar-piece. As fortune would have it, he fell from the scaffolding and received such serious injuries he was brought home only to die.

Murillo is best known for his religious paintings, although many other fine examples of his work deal with realistic subjects, such as the *Spanish Flower Girl*. His most notable achievement is perhaps his series of eleven pictures for the church and hospital of San Jorge, Seville, known as La Caridad, which he completed in 1671. These compassionate and evocative paintings, illustrating works of mercy taken from the Bible or the lives of the saints, include *Christ Healing the Paralytic at the Pool of Bethesda*. The subject is taken from John, V:2-8: "Now there is at Jerusalem by the sheep market a pool, which is called in the Hebrew tongue Bethesda...."

Murillo's production was considerable, and he had many assistants and followers who imitated his style up through the beginning of the nineteenth century.

Adam van Noort, the Elder 1562-1641 • FLEMISH

CHRIST CALLING TO HIM THE LIT-TLE CHILDREN, *Royal Museums of Fine Arts, Brussels, pages 114-115.*

Lambert van Noort of Amesfort reputedly died in great misery. A moderately successful painter of stained glass windows and domestic genre scenes, his life ended when his son Adam was only nine.

Adam van Noort continued in his father's craft, a tradition that would be carried on when Adam's sons, Jan and Adam the Younger, grew up to be painters. He went to Italy when a young man; returning, he became a master in the Guild and painted many works for the churches of Antwerp. He also took on a number of students, including Rubens and Jordaens; the latter eventually became his son-in-law.

Today so few works have been ascribed to him that it is assumed numbers of his paintings have been sold as those of his students.

The artist's exaggerated perspective and the sinuous and complicated treatment of the figures in *Christ Calling to Him the Little Children* suggest that van Noort was attracted to Mannerism. This elegant and complex emotionalized style was popular in the early sixteenth century. Revolting against the rationality and clarity of the Renaissance, Mannerist painters exaggerated proportion and movement for their own sake, deliberately creating an involved and ambiguous spatial scheme intended to heighten the emotional impact of their work. These Mannerist elements were the basis of what was later to become Baroque in the work of van Noort's students.

Nicolas Poussin 1594-1665 • FRENCH

THE MASSACRE OF THE INNO-CENTS, *Musee Condé, Chantilly, France, pages 46-47.*

It has been said the art of Nicolas Poussin distilled the spirit of the seventeenth century in its balance and proportion, its rhythmic movement of line and its foundation in reason.

Poussin was born at Villers, a hamlet in the district of Les Andelys in Normandy. At the age of sixteen, he received some instruction from Quentin Varys of Amiens. Two years later, impatient to study in Paris, he left his home secretly. He worked under Duschesne on the decorations for Luxembourg and other chateaux, and then went to Rome. Studying the Classical remains of the city, he modeled figures in relief and produced countless sketches of the ancient Roman monuments. He also became deeply absorbed in the masters of two contrasting schools: Raphael and Titian. From the first, he learned the value of Classical line and form, and rhythm of design, from the second a use of glowing color. From both, he borrowed figures and compositional schemes.

With the support and encouragement of Cardinal Barberini, Poussin proceeded to paint large-scale Biblical, historical and mythological compositions. Cardinal Barberini was called away from Rome, however, on diplomatic work and Poussin frequently became the victim of derision and assault from anti-French Italians (with their accumulated resentment of French attempts to seize and control their country). Finally, he was forced to disguise himself as an Italian, and try to keep his whereabouts unknown. Fortunately, Cardinal Barberini returned to Rome, and Poussin's name and person became safe once more. He came to be popular not only with the 'Barberini circle' but with Cassiano del Pozzo, a wealthy collector who commissioned him to design monuments based on Classical models.

By 1640, Poussin's reputation had spread to Paris. Louis XIII offered him apartments in the Tuileries and the opportunity to paint the walls of the Louvre's Great Gallery if he would return to France; the artist accepted. Poussin produced eight cartoons on sacred subjects for tapestries and pictures to adorn the chapels of the palaces at Fontainebleau and Saint-Germain. He also executed book designs, illustrations and an imposing series of paintings on "The Labours of Hercules" for the Louvre. But Poussin's attachment to Italy prevailed. Decorative painting bored him, and, reputedly disgusted at French ignorance of Classical art, he went back to Italy in 1642—never to return to his native land.

In the years that followed, Poussin produced the works on which his reputation now rests: boldly drawn and softly colored lyrical subjects taken from Roman antiquity and the Christian faith. In these pieces Poussin was receptive to the influence of Renaissance art, always in that aspect which showed a love of Classical forms. His powerful and energetic *Massacre of the Innocents,* for example, betrays the influence of both Michelangelo and Titian. He also painted landscapes, works of a new and greater intellectual harmony and peace. Characteristic are those composed of Classical statuary and architecture seen amidst large, verdant trees. Here Poussin recalls Giorgione, though with this difference: where Giorgione exuded an elusive and subtle grace, Poussin is specific, proportioned and 'quiet like a picture' rather than 'quiet like nature'.

In 1648 the French Academy was founded, basing its teachings on the ideals rediscovered by Poussin. The Academy, however, held these rules in a mold more rigid than any Poussin ever intended, affecting the development of painting in Europe for the next two hundred years.

Poussin died at the age of seventy-one, having received commissions from the leading figures of Italy and France. Although most of the artist's life was spent in Italy, his work reflects the intellectual climate of his own country, forming a parallel to the writings of his contemporaries Corneille and Racine in an expression of faith in reason. It was in a return to literary and elevated subjects expressed through deliberate forms that Poussin, like the famous dramatists, hoped to realize the majesty of his themes.

The artist's style was to be of unusual importance in the subsequent development of French art, not only in a distorted form through the Academicians, but more creatively in the works of Corot and Cezanne, respectively. Poussin's dream-like and structured scenes affected these two nineteenth-century masters in their widely contrasting yet related landscapes, interpretations of nature which would help form the basis of modern painting.

Raphael 1483-1520 • UMBRIAN-FLORENTINE

The painter who most singly typifies the Classical art of the High Renaissance in its ordered equilibrium, idealized naturalness and utter serenity is Raphaello Santi or Sanzio, known simply as Raphael.

Born in the flourishing cultural center of Urbino, he received his first instruction in the principles of painting from his father, a painter at the court of the Duke of Urbino. His father sent him to Perugino at Perugia, and Raphael learned with astonishing rapidity to imitate to perfection the sweet, sentimental style of his master. In fact, when Perugino went to Florence in 1502, Raphael remained behind and successfully handled the commissions for religious paintings. He was then twenty. Already, his painting displayed the serenity for which he is famous, with clear, light colors and, like his master, a flair for perspective in landscape and architectural backgrounds.

Raphael moved to Florence in 1504, after helping Pinturicchio with the decorations for

THE PROPHET ISAIAH, *(detail),* *Church of San Agostino, Rome,* *pages* 12-13.

the library of Pius II in Siena. Here, a number of influences were to have a lasting effect on his style. He became a friend and admirer of Fra Bartolommeo, from whom he learned what may be called a "grace of design and coloring," as well as the technique of treating drapery in dignified folds. He also studied works of Masaccio and was affected by that artist's strong, full dramatic expression. Finally, he was both awed and inspired by Leonardo, who was working in Florence in 1507-08.

Leonardo's subtleties of modeling and softness of expression were attempted by Raphael. The smiling beauty of the female face became the focal point of one Raphael *Madonna and Child* after another, as the painter refined his composition and shading of color, through the years 1505-1508. He made of each of these works a harmonious and balanced whole, a distillation of quiet beauty.

Being of an essentially gentle nature himself, and reputedly kind to everyone, Raphael had many friends. One of these, Bramante, the architect of St. Peter's, persuaded Pope Julius II to entrust Raphael with the decoration of new rooms at the Vatican. In late 1508, Raphael moved to Rome and began work. His success prompted the Pope to find more assignments for Raphael and, at the Pope's insistence, he repainted walls already covered with frescoes by Piero della Francesca, Andrea del Castagno and his own teacher, Perugino.

Shortly thereafter, when Leo X became the new Pope, Raphael was made director of all the architectural and artistic departments of St. Peter's and the Vatican. He succeeded Bramante, at the latter's request, as the architect of St. Peter's, but progress was too slow for him to leave much mark on its overall design. Yet he designed ornaments, stairways and loggias of considerable splendor. He lived, too, in great luxury and his canvases of this period reflect the grandeur which surrounded him. Exposed to Michelangelo, his 'rival,' Raphael's work developed breadth, scale and power. Vasari, the celebrated biographer of the great Italian painters, tells this story as an example of the Florentine's influence on Raphael: when Michelangelo was away in Florence, Bramante, who had been entrusted with the key to the as yet unfinished Sistine Chapel, admitted Raphael for a look at Michelangelo's work in progress. Raphael then returned to his own half-finished painting, *The Prophet Isaiah* for the Church of San Agostino, and re-worked it with Michelangelo-like power and monumentality.

Raphael was later commissioned to design ten large tapestries for this same Sistine Chapel, which he completed in 1520. That same year he died suddenly, following a short fever, at the age of thirty-seven.

In the work of his seventeen or eighteen years, everything for which fifteenth-century painters had been striving came to a peak. In Raphael, nothing seems accidental or casual. His perfect compositions placed every gesture, every detail in clear and balanced relation to the whole. The problems of the Renaissance were now solved, stated in their most complete and pure form. After this, painting would have to find a new direction.

Rembrandt van Rijn 1606-1669 • DUTCH

In the seventeenth century the Calvinist republic of the United Netherlands produced an extraordinary number of paintings. The prosperity of the country had never been higher. A large, materially-minded middle class purchased art in a quantity previously unheard of, and this new class of patrons also determined the size and style of painting. The artist most associated with this period—Rembrandt van Rijn—was a man who rose above and then fell below this class, and in his life and art, broke its every convention.

The complex and absorbing story of his life begins in Leyden, where his father was a relatively prosperous miller, and where Rembrandt was born. In 1620, Rembrandt prepared himself briefly for a career in law at the University of Leyden, but against his father's wishes he threw it over to devote himself to art. First studying with a painter named van Swanenburg, Rembrandt received further training from Pieter Lastman in Amsterdam. Lastman specialized in Biblical and mythological scenes, and Rembrandt borrowed his teacher's compositions in his earliest works. Even in maturity, this was a common habit with Rembrandt: he would transpose a scene from Titian or Raphael, yet the transposition was always more of a transformation.

Rembrandt's paintings and etchings are charged with an intense search for the mastery of the rhythm and flow of light. Some of his early sketches seem almost abstract in their denial of the shapes of trees, of houses, of streams, yet they capture instantaneously the essential nature of things. With people, he probed underlying character and motivation. He studied his own face so often that he completed over sixty self-portraits. Rembrandt's total work give the impression that he never finished exploring ways of revealing the infinite complexity of man. His mother and his sister frequently sat for him, as did acquaintances and strangers in both Amsterdam and Leyden, where he returned after his years of study. By 1625, at the astonishingly young age of nineteen, he had his own studio; by 1628, several pupils. It was not long before Rembrandt was known as one of the most gifted portrait painters in Leyden.

In 1631, he settled permanently in Amsterdam. Three years later he married Saskia van Uylenburgh, the rich cousin of an art dealer. With this sudden turn in his social and financial status, Rembrandt's life changed dramatically. He began living on a lavish scale; more significantly, he was freed of the necessity of pandering to contemporary tastes in art. He could continue his experiments.

Influenced by Rubens, by Tintoretto and by Titian (all of whose work was widely collected in Northern Europe), Rembrandt instinctively sought out the dramatic potentialities of a growing range of subject matter, giving to the work of his early period a Baroque flavor. Traveling theatre companies making their way through Amsterdam, probably found Rembrandt both in the audience and at the 'stage door', hoping to beg, borrow or buy an exotic costume, a headpiece, an ornament. Rembrandt's fantastic imagination then made the most of these materials in his studio, where he would stage the clemency of a Roman emperor, or paint Saskia as the Roman goddess of war.

Rembrandt's sense of the dramatic was also developed outside the make-believe world of the theatre. Three of his four children died in infancy, a tragedy that multiplied when Saskia died in 1642. These events set into motion a number of changes in his art and fortunes.

In the year of Saskia's death, he had completed a commissioned picture called *The Night Watch*. A daring innovation for a group business portrait, it illuminated certain principals in the foreground, while other figures in the back were visible only in a rather subdued light. Whether the picture displeased the bourgeoisie of Amsterdam as much as legend has it, is disputable. But Rembrandt's commissions definitely declined in the years that followed. This decrease might be explained by the fact that after Saskia's death, Rembrandt's previously acceptable style developed more radical unorthodox elements. Increasingly, clothing and ornament became subsidiary. The artist's earlier dramatizations of violent emotion and physical force were now replaced by quiet scenes with an obscurity and darkness that was not only unprecedented but must have been unpopular. No longer were faces recognizably painted and literally defined; they emerged sometimes half-completed from a mysterious, undefined setting. It has been said Rembrandt "painted the air," and beginning in these years, the artist filled the space of each canvas with an ominous background, usually of a deep golden brown hue. From this background, brilliant circles of intense light—sometimes emanating from the face of the subject, sometimes from behind—offset his subjects with ghost-like power, creating a distinctive mood that commands the attention of the observer.

Throughout his life, but especially from 1639 to 1661, Rembrandt produced an extraordinary quantity of religious work. He read his Bible avidly, and responded to the events and meaning of Christ's ministry with a flood of etchings and oils. The etchings were popular, but except for some Catholic families, the paintings found few buyers. In this large body of work, a unique document of an artist's faith, Rembrandt examined the question of man's existence and purpose on the earth with personal feeling and increasing insight.

In spite of the cool public reception to his change in style, Rembrandt continued to expand and develop in new directions. In the 1650's, he painted with thicker and heavier strokes, depicting objects in a free and bold manner far ahead of his time.

Rembrandt became a father once again in 1654. Hendrickje Stoffels, housekeeper and nurse to Saskia's one remaining son, had become Rembrandt's mistress. Unfortunately, the artist could not marry her; the will left by Saskia did not encourage remarriage, and Rembrandt was increasingly in debt. In 1656 he was forced to declare bankruptcy. Two years later most of his possessions were sold at public auction and the painter moved to a poor section of Amsterdam, populated with many Dutch and Portuguese Jews.

The final years of Rembrandt's life were painful and unhappy, though he continued to receive some commissions. Hendrickje and Rembrandt's son became 'art dealers,' selling both his paintings and etchings. Rembrandt's sympathy and understanding of human experience were now greater than ever. In Christ, Rembrandt found the ideal subject for his theme of man and his conscience. Modeled on young Talmudic students and rabbis, his *Heads of Christ* are among the most powerful and haunting works of his final years, as well as the first depictions of Christ as a Jew.

Rembrandt died at the age of sixty-three, seven years after the death of Hendrickje.

The influence of this Dutch master may be felt in such diverse painters as Velasquez, Goya, Delacroix and van Gogh. The latter wrote: ''And so Rembrandt has alone, or almost alone among painters, that tenderness in the gaze . . . that heartbroken tenderness, that glimpse of a superhuman infinite that seems so natural there.''

Josef de Ribera c.1590-1652 • SPANISH

CHRIST DISPUTING WITH THE DOCTORS, *(detail), Kunsthistorisches Museum, Vienna, pages* 66-67.

Ribera was born of a poor family in the small village of Jativa, on the eastern coast of Spain. His father sent him to nearby Valencia to learn a trade, but he was soon studying painting under Francisco Ribalta, who aroused Ribera's enthusiasm for the naturalistic and dramatic style then evolving in Italy. When only seventeen, Ribera ran off to Rome to study the Italian painters first hand, especially Caravaggio. He profoundly influenced the young Ribera, not only in his painting but in his way of life as well.

The story of Ribera's early years in Italy is typically Romantic: a poor student in a foreign country, he lived on the charity of his comrades, who nicknamed him Lo Spagnoletto, (the little Spaniard). A cardinal, it is said, then took pity on him and attached him to his household, but Ribera soon ran away, declaring that he ''needed the spur of poverty to make him a great artist.'' Ribera's poverty was short lived and, it would seem, not so essential to his greatness. In later years he achieved considerable fame and more than adequate material rewards.

Ribera's financial problems were resolved soon after he moved to Naples. There he made the acquaintance of a rich picture dealer and married his daughter, who brought him both substantial dowry and introductions to the wealthy and sophisticated aristocracy of that city. Naples was then under Spanish rule and Ribera soon ingratiated himself with the Spanish court, enjoying a good share of his countrymen's patronage. He was appointed court painter to the Viceroy and within a few years received frequent commissions from local patrons as well as from the royal court in Spain. The compunctions of his youth were soon forgotten as both wealth and honors poured in on him, and he lived like a grandee —entertaining nobles and princes in his own palace.

Ribera's work has an intensity of dramatic feeling, expressed through sharp, powerful drawing and strong contrast between brilliant colors and dark, mysterious shadows. His figures are simple, human types, for he often used Neapolitan dockhands and fishermen as his models. This desire to bring art back to the world of everyday reality, to represent on canvas the forms and colors of nature in a simple and direct way, had a profound and continuing influence on the course of European painting up to our own time.

Carlo Rosa ?-1678 • ITALIAN

CHRIST BLESSING THE CHILDREN, *(details), Metropolitan Museum of Art, New York, pages* 118-119, 120-121.

Two distinct schools of painting broke into open conflict in seventeenth century Italy. Followers of Caracci, respectful of old masters such as Leonardo and Raphael, sought to return painting to the elegant grace of the classical line. But followers of Caravaggio took pride in a more original approach, based on solid modeling revealed by light, and an acute observation of the world.

Carlo Rosa was born at the height of this conflict, in the village of Bitonto on the southeastern coast of Italy. Coming to Naples, he trained in the sentimental school of Stanzioni, finding himself drawn towards the Caracci-like types in Stanzioni's work; Rosa also admired the pure, elevated approach of Guido Reni. Yet his painting reflects an equally strong leaning to the new realistic trends of the period. Mattia Preti and Gentileschi, artists who copied Caravaggio, probably introduced Rosa to elements of the new style.

Christ Blessing the Children, executed in Naples around 1640, shows an awareness of both schools. It is simple, pure and gentle. Yet there is careful observation of reality in the drawing, directness in the expression of the figure of Christ, and naturalness in the grouping and expressions of the children.

Peter Paul Rubens 1577-1640 • FLEMISH

Analyzing the genius of Rubens, the French philosopher-historian Taine wrote, "no one has gone beyond him in the knowledge of the living organism and of the animal man." This comment on the greatest of all Flemish Baroque masters captures one of the essentials of the Baroque style as a whole.

Rubens was born in Siegen, Westphalia, of Flemish parents. His father, a Calvinist and lawyer, was an exiled official who lived in Cologne until the time of his death. The family returned to Antwerp when Rubens was twelve. There he received a classical education, and was page to a Countess in his spare hours. He began his painting apprenticeship around 1592, studying successively with the landscape painter Verhaecht, Adam van Noort and Van Veen, all established Flemish masters of their day. By 1598, Rubens was listed as a master in the Antwerp Painters Guild of Saint Luke.

The style of his first period, through 1608, is characterized by an alive and intense susceptibility to the influences around him. His travels to Italy began in 1600 and included long stops at Mantua, Genoa and Rome, where he became familiar with the works of Michelangelo and Raphael. When he was a part of the household of the Duke of Mantua, he was sent to Rome to make copies from Raphael for his master. Yet Rubens lived in that period of transition when tastes were changing from the Classical High Renaissance to the Baroque.

In the course of the Renaissance, man discovered more about the physical nature of the human body than had been known previously. Artists began to fill their paintings with outward movement and with inner life: people with real blood pulsating in their veins. Such painters as Titian, and Rubens' contemporary, Caravaggio, extended the versatility of the human form on canvas, and used light in new ways: to hide objects as well as to reveal them, increasing the sense of the mysterious and the dramatic. Rubens was moved by these artists, and, in the period 1609-1614, came to incorporate features of their work in his own painting.

News of his mother's health called him home in 1608. When he arrived in Antwerp, she was dead. He wished to return to Italy but was overruled by his sovereigns, Albrecht and Isabella, who persuaded him to take up permanent residence in the Belgian provinces. In 1609 he married, settled in Antwerp, and established a large studio with many pupils. His output was so increased by these students and hired assistants that his studio has been called a 'factory.' He was well paid, and enjoyed many luxuries. Church commissions filled a great deal of his time, and thus Rubens began to paint scenes from the life of Christ. His paintings often showed unusual narrative action, with a handling of light that may be fairly attributed to the influence of Caravaggio. Many of his subjects were still centrally placed, subordinated to the composition of the whole but his subjects "began to speak." In the words of Taine, "not only the whole face, but the entire attitude conspires to manifest the flowing stream of their thought, feeling and complete being; we hear the inward utterance of their emotion."

Battle, hunt and abduction scenes, often with mythological backgrounds began to interest him about 1614. These subjects freed him further, and gave way to what is known as Rubens' third period, from 1614 to 1622.

In these years Rubens' canvases were filled increasingly with action and movement. His humans seemed to take on the vitality of his animals from the earlier period. At this time, too, his canvases were often gigantic in scale. He wrote to a friend in 1621, "the large size of a picture gives us painters more courage to represent our ideas with the utmost freedom and semblance of reality . . . I confess myself to be, by a natural instinct, better fitted to execute works of the largest size." Baroque churches were well suited to his feelings, for

THE APOSTLE ANDREW, *Prado, Madrid, page* **99.**

THE APOSTLE PETER, *(detail), Prado, Madrid, page* **100.**

THE APOSTLE JOHN, *(detail), Prado, Madrid, page* **101.**

they were decorated according to the newest fashion in Italy: altars magnified to the size of monuments, sometimes reaching to the roofs, with pictures executed on a scale hitherto unknown in order to fit into these surroundings. Rubens finished thirty-nine ceiling panels for the church of Saint Charles in Antwerp in 1620. It was an all-consuming undertaking, tragically destroyed by fire in 1718.

The religious paintings of these years which remain today show the full influence of the Protestant faith which converted Rubens from Catholicism. Christ is depicted as human, suffering the pain and humiliation of a life on earth, rather than as the son of God. The canvases are ablaze with color (often including the use of a bold and vivid red) and striking off-center composition. Allegorical figures are grouped with real figures, the naked with the clothed, and the action set at the most intrinsically dramatic moment.

In all the artist's later work, color was used not merely to fill in form, but rather as if it carried its own specific emotional value. There is also a strange tendency to emphasize the varying qualities of human flesh. Comments Taine: For Rubens, "flesh is a changeable substance in a constant state of renewals. And such, more than any other, is the Flemish body, lymphatic, sanguine and voracious . . . nobody has depicted its contrasts in stronger relief, nor as visibly shown the decay and bloom of life."

Rubens' paintings became somewhat less rich and flamboyant, in the period after 1622. He completed many international commissions, including twenty-four works for the Luxembourg Palace in Paris. Four years after his wife's death, in 1630, he married a sixteen year old girl. But he was less and less in residence at his huge home in Antwerp. In 1633, Flanders was restored to Spanish rule, and Rubens, both before and after this date, served as an ambassador with diplomatic missions on the highest level. While in Spain, he was commissioned to paint several portraits of the King and the Royal family. Meanwhile, in England, Charles I beckoned him to be knighted. The output of his studio continued at an extraordinary rate in his final years—while his style underwent further change: the solid, structural modeling of his third period were now replaced by loose, gracefully flowing compositions of a certain stateliness. In addition to large decorative commissions, Rubens now tried his hand at landscapes, most of which were done on his country estate during the last five years of his life.

At the core of Rubens' work is an awareness of the Flemish and Italian developments in art of the late fifteenth and sixteenth centuries. His fusion of Flemish realism with the Classical tradition of the Renaissance as practiced in Italy, marks a final statement on a great period in painting. Yet this summation is also an introduction to the seventeenth century: powerful, exuberant, sensuous and theatrical.

Jan Swart van Groeningen 1469-1535 · DUTCH

JOHN THE BAPTIST, (detail), Alte Pinakothek, Munich, pages 76-77.

So little is known about Jan Swart or 'le noir Jean' (Black John) as he is sometimes called, that even the years in which he lived are widely disputed. Some claim he was born about 1500 and that he died after 1553; others give the dates listed above. He is thought to have studied with Jan van Scorel (1475-1562), although it is possible van Scorel was his student.

It is known only that Swart was a native of Groeningen, in the Netherlands, taught in nearby Gouda, and lived a few years in Italy. Antwerp is generally acknowledged to be the place of his death.

The birth of landscape painting as a separate genre had not yet taken place in the early sixteenth century. Yet Swart was certainly one of its forerunners. The German, Altdorfer, Swart's contemporary, had begun extending the realm of religious painting to include landscapes with an unusual depth and dramatic feeling. His Biblical scenes take place in vast, fantastic German forests with the trees serving not merely as background for the action, but becoming the dominant element of the painting. This new concept of the world of nature, with man only a part, was an inevitable outgrowth of the scientific, intellectual exploration which began in the Renaissance.

In Swart's *John the Baptist,* John is no more important than the other figures in the painting—all are reduced in size, and the background has assumed an importance equal to them. Yet there is more here: rather than a realistically-observed Dutch landscape, the scene is probably a German or Alpine setting, remembered from his travels to and from Italy.

Dark and moody, a feeling of magic and wonder is created, suggesting a mythical country. The faces and costumes of the people are, however, contemporary, Dutch and realistic.

Swart was a painter far ahead of his time. Not until one hundred years later did the famous landscape painter Lorrain conceive of making the theme and subject of a painting totally subordinate to landscape. And it was not until the late nineteenth century that Vincent van Gogh gave a totally subjective expressiveness to landscape, reflecting a wide range of emotional colors.

Otto van Veen 1558-1629 • FLEMISH

Although born at Leyden in the Netherlands Otto van Veen is considered a Flemish painter. His father, a burgomaster when Holland was under Spanish Catholic rule, was forced to flee the country with his family when the forces of Protestantism swept through his town.

Thus, young van Veen's early days were spent traveling from one city in Flanders to another, until his father finally settled in Liege. At eighteen he was sent by the Prince Bishop of Liege to Rome. Here he remained five years, studying the art of religious and portrait painting with Zuccaro.

Returning to Liege, van Veen passed the majority of the years that followed in the aristocratic environment of Europe's courts. The Archbishop of Liege dispatched him on a mission to Rudolph II in Vienna. In 1585 he was appointed court painter to Alexander Farnese, Governor of the Low Countries. Five years later he settled in Antwerp, becoming painter to the court of Archduke Albert and Isabel, and in 1612 he was made Master of the Mint.

His activities were as numerous and varied as his travels. He designed prints for books and engaged in teaching—the most notable of his pupils being Peter Paul Rubens.

THE CALLING OF THE APOSTLE ANDREW, *(detail), Church of Saint Andrew, Antwerp, pages* **96-97.**

Marten de Vos 1532-1603 • FLEMISH

Born in Antwerp in 1532, Marten was the son of Pieter de Vos, a competent but undistinguished painter from whom he received his first training as an artist. At the age of twenty-three he went to Italy, the goal of young and aspiring painters from all of Europe. He studied in Rome for a number of years and, fascinated by the works of the Venetians which he saw there, he gravitated to Venice. He soon gained the friendship of Tintoretto, the most dramatic and powerful of the contemporary Venetians, and became his assistant, painting many of the landscape portions of that painter's vast and turbulent compositions. De Vos learned a great deal from Tintoretto and although his talent was markedly inferior to that of his master, he became quite skillful, especially as a colorist, and was commissioned to do both historical works and portraits of many of the most illustrious Italian families, including some of the Medici.

After five years he returned to Flanders to find that his Italian reputation had preceded him. Antwerp was then the great seaport of Northern Europe with as many as five hundred ships a day loading and unloading goods from all over the world at its docks, and over a thousand foreign merchants in residence. This commercial prosperity naturally led to increased cultivation of the arts, and de Vos found himself much in demand. He received many commissions, both to do altarpieces for the affluent churches of Antwerp and its environs, and portraits of the wealthy merchants and guildsmen of the city.

JESUS TEACHING HIS DISCIPLES, *(detail), Schloss Kapelle, Celle, Germany, pages* **86-87.**

THE TRIBUTE MONEY, *(detail of Peter), Royal Museum of Fine Arts, Antwerp, page* **90.**

THE WIDOW'S MITE, *(detail), Royal Museum of Fine Arts, Antwerp, page* **92.**

Rogier van der Weyden 1399-1464 • FLEMISH

In the last half of the fifteenth century when the fame of Flemish painting spread throughout Europe and into Italy, one name was linked with that of Jan van Eyck as the greatest of his time: Rogier van der Weyden. Although his reputation suffered an eclipse until the last century, he is today considered one of the luminaries of European painting. He ranks as a supreme craftsman in the rendering of visual appearances with an almost tangible

ANNUNCIATION, *(detail), Alte Pinakothek, Munich, page* **17.**

**TRIPTYCH OF CHRIST, THE VIR-
GIN AND ST. JOHN THE EVAN-
GELIST,** *(left wing) John The
Baptist (detail), The Louvre,
Paris, pages* **74-75.**

DESCENT FROM THE CROSS, *(detail of mourners), The Prado,
Madrid, pages* **132-133.**

naturalism, as well as one of the great portrayors of human pathos, revealed with a deep and strange expressive power.

The early years of Rogier's career are somewhat mysterious. He was born in Tournai in 1399, and for the next twenty-five years nothing is known of him. Then suddenly, in 1426, a certain Rogelet de la Pasture (the French equivalent of Rogier van der Weyden) was honored by the Burgomaster of Tournai and presented with eight measures of wine—twice the quantity awarded to the great Jan Van Eyck on a similar occasion. He must, therefore, already have been an artist of some importance, and is referred to as Master Rogier in a contemporary document. Yet the next year 'Rogelet de la Pasture' was taken on by the most famous local painter, Robert Campin, as an apprentice. This seeming ambiguity may be the result of his having obtained his previous mastership in some other craft, possibly that of goldsmith or sculptor, or that he had been made master in another town. In any event, he was made master in Louvain in 1432, but he worked there only a few years. He had moved to nearby Brussels by 1435, where he became Town Painter.

A flourishing and wealthy commercial city, Brussels was also the frequent residence of the court and was thus a favorable environment for craftsmen and painters. Among his patrons Rogier soon numbered bankers, merchants, ecclesiasts and other wealthy crafts-men, as well as the Duke of Burgundy and the Duchess of Brabant. One of his first recorded commissions, from the Society of Cross-Bowmen of his native Louvain, was for the renowned *Descent from the Cross.* Mary of Hungary bought the painting when she was serving as regent of the Netherlands, and sent it to Spain for her brother, the Emperor Charles V. It was immediately admired and the first of many copies to be made of it appeared in 1443, only five years after its completion. Rogier's fame soon spread abroad and in 1449 he made a trip to Italy, partly for the celebration of the Holy Year in Rome, but also at the invitation of the influential d'Este family. In Italy he admired the works of Gentile da Fabriano, but was, in turn, admired by the Italians—who must have been overwhelmed by his Flemish technique with its naturalistic detail, as well as by his sensitive and acute psychological characterization.

Rogier's work had a profound influence on all Flemish painting and echoes of his themes and figures appear over and over in the work of succeeding generations of painters. He invented a whole vocabulary of expressions and gestures which do not literally describe the emotions but symbolize and ennoble them. This removal of the emotions into a plane beyond the ephemeral world of reality, combined with the isolation of the figures in an almost abstract space, give to Rogier's work a tragic grandeur.

SAINT LUKE PAINTING THE VIRGIN, *(detail) by Rogier van der Weyden, Alte Pinakothek, Munich*

ACKNOWLEDGMENTS

DANIEL W. JONES and RHODA GRADY, Special Projects Research Directors for the National Broadcasting Company, whose tireless search for paintings through museums and private collections far and near made possible the television production *The Coming of Christ,* and whose cooperation and generous assistance have helped immeasurably in the task of completing this book.

All the museums, galleries and collections who have generously consented to permit their paintings to be reproduced; also, the trustees of the Chatsworth Settlement, England, for permission to reproduce the drawing of the Madonna and Child by Raphael; St. Mark's Library of General Theological Seminary, New York, for permission to reproduce the map from the early King James Bible; the Phaidon Press Ltd., London, for permission to quote from Bernard Berenson's, *Italian Painters of the Renaissance* (distributed in the U.S. by the New York Graphic Society, Greenwich, Conn.); The Frick Art Reference Library, The Print Room and Picture Collection of The New York Public Library, and the Drawing Collection of The Metropolitan Museum of Art for their invaluable research facilities and expert and cooperative staffs; Esther Leonhardt and Milton Wassner of Camera Clix, Inc. and Max G. Lowenherz of Three Lions, Inc. for making their files available; special thanks to W. H. Lovelock, Esq. of Rayant Pictures, Ltd. for his services in obtaining permissions from England, and to The American Bible Society for assistance in research on Biblical maps.

The majority of photographs in this book were commissioned by NBC especially for *The Coming of Christ.* The remainder have been supplied by the museums and by the following agencies and publishers: Harry N. Abrams, Inc.; Black Star Publishing Company (agents for Conzett & Huber, Switzerland); Camera Clix, Inc.; Freelance Photographers Guild, Inc.; Three Lions, Inc.; The Bettmann Archive; and Paul Bitjebier of Brussels.

INDEX TO THE PAINTINGS

THE TEXT for *The Coming of Christ* was drawn directly from the King James version of the Holy Scriptures. Verses were selected and arranged to aid the narrative flow, with transitional passages added for clarity and amplification.

THE PHOTOGRAPHS AND PAINTINGS were chosen for their unique ability to dramatize and express the *spirit* of the text. Thus, strict adherence to the subject matter of certain paintings has been modified to permit the use of selected details to illustrate a particular moment or event in the life and teaching of Christ.